MAINE'S MILITARY MIGHT

MEMORIES OF MILITARY INFRASTRUCTURE IN THE PINE TREE STATE

AREND T. THIBODEAU

AMERICA
THROUGH
TIME

America Through Time®
An imprint of Sutton Publishing Inc.
www.through-time.com

First published 2025

ISBN 978-1-63499-567-2

Typeset in 10pt on 13pt Sabon
Printed and bound in the United States of America

PREFACE

As a third-generation veteran and a lifelong resident of Maine, it seems only natural that my writing and research have taken me down a path exploring Maine's military history. It all began for me in earnest during 2023 when I was researching my book *The Aroostook Arms Race: Cold War in the Crown of Maine*. The more I researched, the more I came to realize just how significant Maine's military past is and how significant our quiet little state has been in the strategic role of defending the United States.

Even before Maine was a state, the Battle of Machias was one of the earliest naval battles of the American Revolutionary War, and it brought to light the importance of maritime warfare and coastal defenses. Maine's significance as a coastal defensive position became apparent early on; however, Maine's coastal locations did not host maritime defenders alone. On land, the U.S. Army has protected our rocky shores and inland locations alike. The U.S. Army also defended our skies until the creation of the U.S. Air Force, which then also defended the skies over the Pine Tree State.

From the rocky coast to the northern potato fields, and from the western mountains to the blueberry barrens down east, at one time or another throughout the state's history, the various branches of the military have established a presence throughout the entire state and the list of Maine forts, strongholds, depots, and stations is long. Even before Maine realized its sovereignty as a state, it defended its borders against England, France, Spain, and then the Confederacy during the American Civil War.

As a state, Maine played a significant role in both World War I and World War II. After World War II, the Cold War began, which would redefine the United States' position on the world stage. During the Cold War, the strategic location of the state was a first line of defense against the threat of a Soviet nuclear strike—both from the skies and the seas, where Soviet bombers, missiles, and submarines armed with thermonuclear weapons were a constant perceived threat. Suffice to say, Maine has played a huge role in the defense of the United States for the nation's entire history.

With that said, this is just a glimpse into the military history of Maine and its defensive position as a state. The locations which I have selected, I have also visited. As I explored the various locations, I tried to photograph what I could of anything that is left, and I have attempted to present it in a way that best represents what these places once were. I have also included historic photos and information that best represents the significant histories of these locations. Some of these locations have an abundance of historic photos, documents, and mission information, while others have very little. The same can be said of the artifacts or evidence of these places that have been left behind.

CONTENTS

DEDICATIONS AND ACKNOWLEDGEMENTS

This book is dedicated to the men and women of the United States Armed Forces, past and present.

Also, my grandfather, Donald H. Hardwick, who served in the United States Coast Guard from 1942–1945.

During his time aboard the USCGC *Campbell*, he served as first loader on one of the ship's 5-inch, 51-caliber guns and was off the coast of Saipan when the atomic bombs were dropped on Hiroshima and Nagasaki. Before the surrender of Germany, the *Campbell* also worked as an armed escort during the Battle of the Atlantic, sinking a German U-boat in 1943. One of my grandfather's shipmates on board the *Campbell* was Sinbad, the ship's mascot who served from 1937–1948, and held the non-commissioned rank of Chief Dog (K9C).

This book is also dedicated to my father, Arnold G. Thibodeau, who served in the United States Army from 1966–1968. His time in Vietnam while assigned to the 519th Military Intelligence Battalion left a profound impact on him that continues to this day. I admire both my father's and grandfather's courage, and I thank them for their service and sacrifices.

I would like to thank my wife, Christine, who proudly served in the United States Army, and whose invaluable research played a significant role in the development of this book.

And I wish to extend my gratitude to Charlie Cormier, Leigh E. Cummings Jr., the Cary Library, Kennebec Historical Society, Maine Aviation Museum, Maine Historical Society, Maine Historic Preservation Commission, and the MITRE corporation for their assistance during the research of this book.

Sinbad the sailor dog. He would be at morning muster every day with the crew, lifejacket in mouth, which he would drop to bark once his name was called at role. According to Coast Guard historians, during the ship's attack which sank the German submarine, Sinbad "snoozed through the entire attack."[1,2]

INTRODUCTION

During the early nineteenth century in the region known as Maine, strategists became profoundly aware of the area's lack of formidable defenses following the War of 1812. While the area that would become Maine was still part of Massachusetts' territory, Congress approved the creation of multiple forts, arsenals, and armories known as the "Third System" in United States' fortifications development. The bill was passed in 1816, but it would take decades to come to fruition.

Four years later, in 1820, Maine separated from Massachusetts and achieved statehood. Having no clear northern border, tensions with British-controlled Canada created border disputes with Maine, which led to the development of the Kennebec Arsenal in 1828. In addition, fortifications along Maine's largely unprotected coast were built in the years preceding the Civil War and were used in the state's defense until the end of World War II, after which they were mostly abandoned.

Then in 1948, events following the end of World War II led to the Cold War which lasted more than four decades and brought a whole new line of defenses to the State of Maine. This time, emphasis was placed on defending the nation in a nuclear world. As technology progressed, so did the methods of warfare as United States military defenses went from cannonballs and gunpowder to thermonuclear warheads and long-range aircraft, bringing with them the ability to wipe out entire cities with the drop of a bomb or launching of a missile. During the nuclear buildup of the Cold War, Maine saw the development of radar bases, missile launch facilities, a naval air station, two U.S. Air Force heavy bomber bases, communications stations, and more.

Join me as I explore the history of some of these once active facilities, sharing their unique stories and explaining why they were selected as places of strategic importance in the defense of the United States. Some of these locations are now protected as places of historical significance in the defense of Maine and the nation, while others have been forgotten and abandoned and are quickly being reclaimed by nature. The places I have selected are by no means a conclusive list, nor are they any more significant than any places which I have unintentionally excluded.

1
MAINE FORTIFIES

After the sacking and burning of Washington, D.C., in 1814, the vulnerabilities of the United States were left profoundly exposed. Despite the United States' "First System" of defense buildup under President Washington in 1794 and the "Second System" during President Jefferson's administration in 1807, the ability of the British Royal Navy to access the nation's capital via the Chesapeake Bay led the administration of President James Madison to create the "Third System" of defense fortifications.

Although it would take years to create these defensive positions, President Madison appointed a board of engineers to design the fortifications which were to be made of much more durable materials than previous systems' wooden or brick and mortar designs. However, as it would turn out, methods of warfare and advances in weaponry were quickly outpacing the construction and durability of these defenses.

During his second inaugural address in 1821, President Madison spoke of the fortification buildup of the new system which was in the planning and early development stages:

> By these fortifications, supported by our navy, to which they would afford like support, we should present to other powers an armed front from the St. Croix to the Sabine, which would protect, in the event of war, our whole coast and interior from invasion: an even in the wars of other powers, in which we were neutral, they would be found eminently useful, as, by keeping their public ships at a distance from our cities, peace and order in them would be preserved, and the government be protected from insult.[1]

At first, facilities that were built during the "Second System" were reinforced and redeveloped. This included such forts on the Maine coast as Fort Scammell on House Island and Fort Preble in South Portland, which were built to protect Portland and Casco Bay; both are forts that saw military action while they were active.

Fort Scammell and a British privateer are said to have traded shots during the War of 1812, but no further shooting took place and neither shot connected. As the story goes, the privateer attempted to abscond with a private vessel when the would-be thief was fired upon by the fort's watch.[2] The British brigand returned fire, and the anti-climactic tale ends there as the mysterious marine marauder disappeared into the night.

Fort Preble saw action during the American Civil War at the Battle of Portland Harbor when soldiers from Fort Preble, along with civilian volunteers, captured twenty-three Confederate soldiers who had stolen the United States Revenue Cutter *Caleb Cushing* from its Portland Harbor berth. The commandeering confederates were ultimately captured, but not before setting fire to the cutter which resulted in an explosion that shook the city of Portland as 500 pounds of powder in the cutter's hold ignited, obliterating the Federal vessel. The prisoners were then taken to Fort Preble and held until they were able to be transferred to confinement in Boston.[3]

Fort Preble also hosted the only Maine soldier to be executed in the state during the Civil War. Private Billy Laird was executed for desertion at the fort on July 15, 1863, and was the only soldier to be executed on Maine soil during the Civil War.

Private Laird was court-martialed in Augusta for deserting the 17th Maine Infantry Regiment on July 2, 1863. The unit he deserted was at the Battle of Gettysburg defending Cemetery Ridge on the day of his court-martial. He was found guilty and sentenced to death by firing squad.[4]

In a twist of cruel irony, the commander of the Army Department of the East, General John Wool, ordered a stay of execution pending a presidential review. Unfortunately, riots in New York had disrupted telegraph communications, and the general's order arrived at the fort hours too late—the private had been executed. In his book *Red Diamond Regiment*, historian and author Professor William B. Jordan wrote that Laird was said to have been "lacking common intelligence," so it might be safe to assume the general's failed request was out of concern for the young soldier's mental state.[5]

Fort Gorges on Hog Island Ledge in Casco Bay was a "Third System" fort that was intended to be built to support neighboring Fort Preble and Fort Scammel, but construction was not authorized by Congress until 1857, and the raising of the fort did not start until 1858. Construction was accelerated when the Civil War broke out in 1861, but the fort was not complete until the end of the war in 1865. At the time construction was finished, the fort only consisted of two stories, rather than the original three-story facility that was planned.

The fort was never manned as its construction and armaments were soon outdated by military advancements that were made throughout the Civil War (such as rifled guns and steel-sided ships). Fort Gorges' only use was during World War II when the fort was a storage site for mines that were used for the protection of Casco Bay.

Further up the coast from Fort Gorges, Fort Popham was built at the same location as a small "Second System" battery in Phippsburg and located at a narrow and strategic location at the mouth of the Kennebec River. Defenses here would prevent advancing enemy ships from entering the river and attacking the capital city of Augusta, the Kennebec Arsenal, or the shipyards in Bath. Like Fort Gorges, Fort Popham was built during the Civil War; it was never fully completed when it was manned during the final ten months of the war.

Fort Popham and its more than forty cannons were obsolete by the time the Civil War ended, but fortification reinforcements that occurred during the Endicott Program saw the fort transform into a facility to maintain controlled minefields throughout the Spanish-American War and World War I; during the latter war, the fort was garrisoned by personnel of the Coast Defenses of Portland.

The forts I have listed in this chapter are a very small sampling of the fortifications that were built on the coast of Maine during the "Third System" of United States fortification, but they remained significant into the twentieth century and throughout World War II. We will return to these locations in Chapter 5.

A once-classified aerial view of Fort Preble with its artillery batteries, *c.* 1936. Note: Spring Point Ledge Lighthouse is at the top of the photo in the center.[6]

The outer wall remnants of Fort Preble which is now the campus for Southern Maine Community College; many of the fort's original buildings are still in use by the school. Spring Point Light is now a tourist attraction, a breakwater was added in 1951, and guided tours of the historic lighthouse are offered. Note: Fort Gorges in the background to the left and Fort Scammel is directly across from the lighthouse.

This is a closer view of Fort Gorges. It is a snapshot I took as I was riding the ferry to Great Diamond Island to visit Fort McKinley.

Fort Popham's tidal moat at the back of the fort looking toward the mouth of the river. Small arms portals run down the side, and you can just see the arches of the casemates on the upper level.

Interior Fort Popham on the second floor. The Third System construction is impressive looking down through the interior. This perspective is looking down the cannon casemates which you can see to the right of each interior arch.

The granite work in all of Maine's Third System forts is remarkable, these spiral stairs between Fort Popham's first and second floors have held up well for over 160 years.

2
KENNEBEC ARSENAL

During the early days of Maine's statehood, territory disputes between Maine and British-controlled Canada were robust. When tensions began escalating in the mid-1820s, the U.S. Army set up a garrison near present-day Houlton and began fortifying the area. Fearing that territorial disputes would evolve into bloodshed, U.S. Army defense forces were rightfully concerned that the closest arsenal (where they could be dispatched munitions) was in Massachusetts, some 200 miles away. Knowing that British forces from Canada could descend from the north and the British Navy could attack from the sea, potentially cutting off Maine, the building of fortifications and an arsenal was of paramount concern.

In 1828, construction began on the Kennebec Arsenal located along the Kennebec River in Maine's capital of Augusta. Legislature's final signing of the bill which allowed for the construction of the facility occurred on March 3, 1827, ten days after Augusta was designated the state's capital.[1] Located on 40 acres, on a gently sloping bank along the Kennebec River, a large arsenal complex, barracks building, guard house, magazines, and officers' quarters were constructed from granite taken from the nearby Hallowell quarry; various other wooden structures made the arsenal complex complete.

By the time border tensions culminated in the bloodless Aroostook War in 1838, the Kennebec Arsenal was able to supply munitions even though no shots were fired. In addition to the arsenal buildings, a large granite docking area and retaining wall were built along the edge of the river. The impressive three-story main arsenal building was large enough for storage of more than 140,000 muskets and the two powder magazines on the property could store over 800 barrels of powder.

The arsenal remained active throughout the Mexican-American War (1846–1848), during which rockets and fixed ammunition were manufactured at the facility and shipped south to the front. In 1855, seven years after the war ended, an inventory was conducted with more than 24,000 muskets, close to 1,000 tons of gun powder, over 5,400 rounds of cannon shot, and 50,000 pounds of cannon power all listed as being stored at the arsenal.[2]

During the Civil War, the facility manufactured substantial quantities of fixed ammunition. There was such a great demand for paper cartridges, temporary buildings were constructed so that men and women, young and old alike, could expedite the manufacture of ammunition. Records indicate that at one time, the number of arms stored at the arsenal exceeded $1 million in nineteenth-century value (which would be more than $40 million in 2025).[3]

As the twentieth century approached, weapons manufacturing and munitions handling had advanced, and arsenals such as the one in Augusta were becoming antiquated. As the nineteenth century concluded, the arsenal had outlived its usefulness, and its location was a hindrance on the national level. In 1901, the arsenal was abandoned by the U.S. Army except for a small contingent that remained at the post until December 1903 when it was left for good. The complex sat idle until being transferred to the State of Maine to be used as part of the Maine Insane Hospital complex in 1905. The Maine Insane Hospital was eventually renamed the Augusta Mental Health Institute and continued to operate until 2004 when the arsenal property was again abandoned.

A developer from North Carolina bought the property from the State of Maine in 2007 with a promise to develop it into condos, restaurants, and other boutique-style public outlets, but the property was neglected and fell into disrepair. Maine Preservation (a Maine-based non-profit) listed the arsenal on its 2013 Most Endangered Properties list, and the State of Maine was left no choice but to file suit against the developer in a 2013 lawsuit.[4] The lawsuit was ultimately dropped with the developer's promise and agreement to make improvements to the property.[5] However, only the bare minimum was done to prevent a foreclosure by the state and the facilities continued to decline.

After fifteen years of neglect, the City of Augusta deemed the property dangerous in 2022 due to the many problems that exist such as lead paint, mold infestation and interior decay of the buildings.[6] A new ultimatum was given to the developer who is required to initiate repairs to the buildings, but it remains to be seen what will come of the property which appears to be in peril.

Many historians assert that the Kennebec Arsenal is the nation's best and most complete example of an early nineteenth-century military arsenal. The structures which were built from quarried Maine granite during the "Third System" of fortification development are important pieces of Maine's history as well as United States' military history.

Army field artillery personnel pose with a cannon in front of the main arsenal building, with the officers quarters (quarters two) in the background, *c.* 1900. (*Photo courtesy of the Kennebec Historical Society, Augusta*)

This 2024 image of the arsenal building with the officers' quarters two in the background; photograph taken from a similar perspective as the previous image.

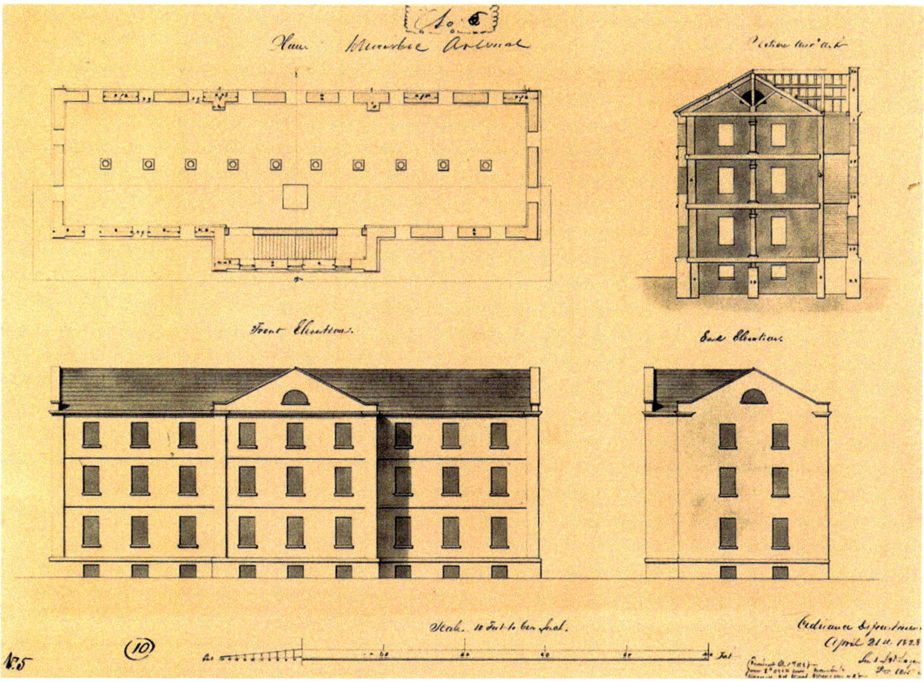

An original sketch/drawing of the main arsenal building plan, drawn by Lieutenant Julius A. d'Lagnel, dated April 21, 1828.[7]

The main arsenal building with the Augusta State Capital building in the background. Construction on the capital began in 1829 and was built nearly the same time as the arsenal was constructed.

Simon Wing of Waterville created this image in 1858, and it is the earliest known photograph of the Kennebec Arsenal. The structures on the hillside near the flagpole are laboratory buildings. They were replaced by a single laboratory in 1877. (*Photo courtesy of the Maine Historic Preservation Commission*)

No trace of the labs or the flagpole can be seen in 2024. The supermax facility (which is in the far background, on top of the hill) was not part of the arsenal complex and was added by the Maine Insane Hospital in 1908 as a maximum-security residence facility.

A photo taken from the quay along the shore of the river. The 186-year-old granite stonework remains impressive to this day.

The commandant's residence sits on the hill in the background and both officer's quarters flank the main arsenal building in this 2024 image.

From a distance the buildings seem to be in sound condition, but as you approach them for closer inspection, years of neglect become quite apparent.

3
MAINE ENTERS THE WORLD STAGE

Aside from both the American-Indian War and American Civil War, it can be reasoned that Maine has always played a part on the world stage, but World War I changed the global landscape significantly. Along with changes in warfare came changes to the United States' importance in global affairs, as well as changes to our defensive positions at home and abroad.

World War I brought new advances in weaponry such as airborne warfare and submarine warfare. Although both types of warfare developed quickly and created constant threats from the sky and seas, it was submarine warfare which emerged as one of the most fearsome types of warfare ever devised and a constant threat to supply shipping lanes in the Atlantic Ocean.

The U.S. Navy was an obvious choice to counteract this type of marine menace, but the United States did not yet have an air force to counteract threats from the skies, so the responsibility of defending the airspace rested primarily with the U.S. Army (although the Navy also had their share of aviators).

In addition, Civil Defense began to organize in communities. The Ground Observer Corps (GOC) was established, recruiting thousands of volunteers to learn how to identify approaching enemy aircraft and hold vigil at established lookout locations, which varied from lookout towers to suburban rooftops—anywhere that offered unobstructed views of possible aerial approaches. Volunteers had to be ready to call in sightings to a filter center who would then determine the threat and response.

When the late 1930s brought the imminent approach of World War II, the Army Corp of Engineers began constructing army airfields around the nation. Two such airfields in Maine were constructed in Presque Isle and Houlton.

Presque Isle and Houlton were both originally constructed as commercial airports, but they became integral parts of the North Atlantic Transport Route for U.S. Army Air Transport Command during World War II. Although Presque Isle would also become a very important and strategic location during the Cold War for both Air Defense Command, and then Strategic Air Command, the Houlton Army Airfield was only used by the Department of Defense (then the U.S. Department of War) during World War II.

4
HOULTON ARMY AIR FORCE BASE

The Houlton Army Air Force Base had humble beginnings as a municipal airport owned by the town of Houlton, but in 1939, all that changed. Adolf Hitler's German forces invaded Poland on September 1, 1939, and two days later, France and England declared war on Germany; Europe was at war. Although the United States were still two years away from entering the war, President Roosevelt felt U.S. participation in a new world war was unavoidable and just a matter of time. The U.S. held the position as a strong advocate for defeating Hitler's Germany and wanted to supply U.S.-built planes to the war effort. However, the Neutrality Act prevented the U.S. from offering direct support to Allied countries at war, so U.S.-made warplanes could not be flown into Canada *en route* to Europe.

It was then decided that to circumvent restrictions caused by the Neutrality Act, planes would be taken to the closest possible point to Canada so they could be transported by land into the neighboring country and expedited to Europe. Houlton was chosen due to its proximity to New Brunswick, and on June 6, 1940, hundreds of spectators witnessed thirty-three Stinson Model 105 trainer planes arrive in Houlton for transport by land into Canada (approximately one-half mile) where they would complete the journey to Europe.

Six days later, on June 12, Curtis SBC-3 "Helldiver" dive-bombers began arriving at the airfield to be pulled the short distance into Canada. This time crowds were restrained, and the operation began to resemble that of a clandestine military operation. In a demonstration of true Yankee ingenuity, most all the planes were pulled by local farmers with tractors after the planes had been flown in by U.S. Navy and Army pilots working under civilian contracts. The planes would be towed the extremely short distance to the Canadian border where they would pass through U.S. and Canadian Customs to be flown from a nearby Canadian airfield. From there they would fly to Halifax and then continue to Europe. It was shortly after these operations began when the Neutrality Act was amended, allowing planes to be flown directly into Canada, but not before a total of eighty-two aircraft were transported in this manner.[1]

In 1941, the United States War Department purchased the airfield from the town of Houlton for $1 with the stipulation that once the current state of emergency had been resolved, Houlton could buy it back, for the same price. Suddenly, construction (which had been progressing slowly) became robust. The War Department also reported it would spend $2,418,000 to build the base and assign 715 military personnel. In a report by the *Houlton Pioneer Times*, construction was described as frantic, stating the airfield was being considered as a ferry base for heavy bomber traffic. Engineers and contractors began working twenty-four hours a day, seven days a week to bring the base to specifications, raising dozens of buildings, two large hangars, and doing extensive runway work, including paving and adding taxiways. Houlton and the region saw expansive growth in a short period of time.[2]

The United States entered the war after it was attacked by Japanese forces at Pearl Harbor on December 7, 1941. On December 11, it was announced by acting commander Maj. Albert C. Holburn that civilians were no longer permitted at the Houlton Air Base and armed guards would be posted at the gates to dissuade civilian traffic from entering the base.[3]

Throughout the nation, a Civil Defense structure organized, forming both the Aircraft Warning Service and the Ground Observer Corps (GOC), and in the Houlton community, the talk of the town was regarding civil defense and air raids. Aircraft observation posts for the GOC were constructed at high points around town and tensions were elevated as citizens worried about threats from the skies.

On December 26, Maj. Holburn assumed command of the Houlton airfield, announcing he would prepare the base for the arrival of the 20th Air Corps Ferrying Squadron which was then activated under his command in March 1942.

In June 1942, the Royal Air Force Ferry Command unit was established at Houlton Army Air Force Base and together the joint commands played a vital role in the Air Transport Command's North Atlantic air ferry route. Aircraft being transported by the RAF Ferry Command, the U.S. Army, and others were serviced and checked by both RAFFC and Army Air Corps personnel before flying to other destinations. In addition, Air Transport Command had regular scheduled cargo flights coming into Houlton, and Northeast Airlines (who had been operating out of the airfield all along) was granted permission to continue passenger flights into the air base; not surprisingly, because most passengers were personnel bound to or from the base. Activities were brisk at Houlton Army Air Force Base and the community of Houlton thrived.

The winters were fierce, and the summers were short. Crews would be required to maintain aircraft in temperatures as low as 25 and 30 below and snowfalls were measured by the foot. The boiler system would work overtime in the hangars just to maintain an interior temperature of 40 degrees. In summer, soldiers were kept conditioned by bivouacking 25 miles southwest of Houlton to Pleasant Lake. The men would have to hike there fully geared in backpacks, then spend a week tenting and conducting field exercises in the Maine wilderness with black flies, mosquitos, and horse flies, all before hiking back home 25 miles to Houlton.[4]

Activities at the air base remained brisk all through 1942 and most of 1943, but in September 1943, things began to change. The RAF Ferry Command unit terminated operations from Houlton and moved its personnel to other locations. It was replaced by a small RAF ferrying squadron which provided fuel and minor repairs to transient RAF aircraft passing through Houlton.

In January 1944, it was announced that operations were going to be curtailed at the Houlton base, and the Houlton Army Airfield was placed on stand-by status, at which point it became an auxiliary airfield for neighboring Presque Isle Army Airfield. In July 1944, U.S. Army infantry personnel were then stationed on the base and a prisoner of war (POW) camp was established. From July 1944 until May 1946, the camp operated as Service Command Unit (SCU) 119 and the 704th MP Battalion.

A total of 1,500 personnel stationed at the airbase contributed immensely to the war effort by assuring the supply chain stayed open in the North Atlantic, during the time when the Battle of the Atlantic raged as the Allied and Axis powers fought from above and below the seas. Well over 3,000 aircraft passed through the Houlton Army Air Force Base during the time it was an active part of Air Service Command/Army Air Transport Command.

Today, the Houlton International Airport plays an active and important role as a hub of commerce and the gateway to Aroostook County. The community had a 2020 population of slightly more than 6,000 people, and despite this being under the 1950 all-time high of 8,377 residents, the community prospers and lives up to its motto: "Valuing the past, planning for the future."

H. Lloyd Child, a chief test pilot, talks with other pilots as they clear U.S. Navy dive-bombers through customs. Collection officer/customs agent John L. Polleys is in uniform, expediting the planes through customs so they may be towed into Canada. (*Image courtesy of Leigh E. Cummings, from the collections of Aroostook County Historical and Art Museum*)

Arnold Peabody, a local farmer, towing a Curtis SBC-3 Helldiver dive bomber to Canada. (*From the collections of Aroostook County Historical and Art Museum. MaineMemory.net, item # 13520*)

After the attack on Pearl Harbor, armed guards would only permit active-duty military personnel to enter the base, and most operations became classified. (*Courtesy Aroostook County Historical and Art Museum*)

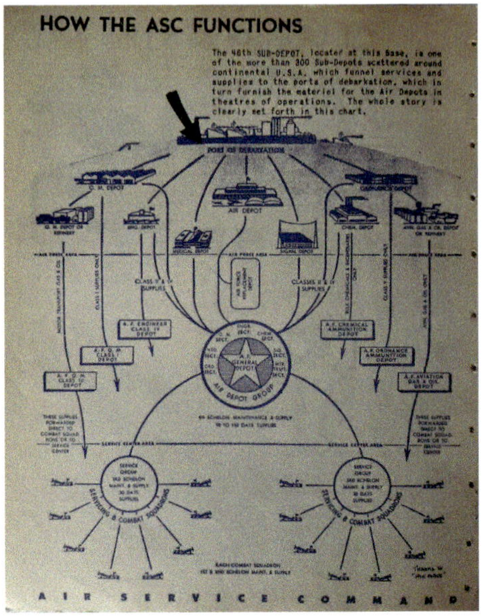

Above left: The Hangar was a weekly publication printed and produced exclusively at the Houlton Army Air Force Base. This weekly news booklet was funded by the post exchange and needed approval from the base public relations office due to the confidential and sensitive nature of base operations. This cover depicts snow removal on the flightline with the control tower in the background. (*Courtesy Aroostook County Historical and Art Museum*)

Above right: The back cover of the May 29, 1943, issue of *The Hangar* depicts a flow chart with the function of the 46th Sub-Depot and how it operates within the Army Air Service Command structure. (*Courtesy Aroostook County Historical and Art Museum*)

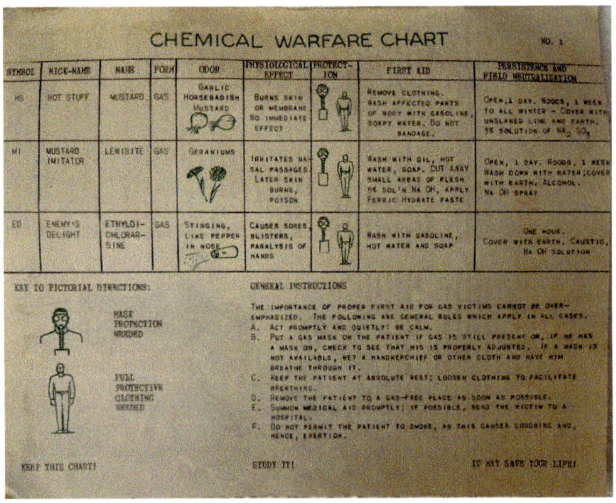

CHEMICAL WARFARE CHART NO. 1

SYMBOL	NICK-NAME	NAME	FORM	ODOR	PHYSIOLOGICAL EFFECT	PROTECTION	FIRST AID	PERSISTENCE AND FIELD NEUTRALIZATION
HS	HOT STUFF	MUSTARD	GAS	GARLIC HORSERADISH MUSTARD	BURNS SKIN OR MEMBRANE NO IMMEDIATE EFFECT		REMOVE CLOTHING. WASH AFFECTED PARTS OF BODY WITH GASOLINE, SOAPY WATER. DO NOT BANDAGE.	OPEN, 1 DAY. WOODS, 1 WEEK TO ALL WINTER – COVER WITH UNSLAKED LIME AND EARTH. 3% SOLUTION OF $NA_2 SO_3$
MI	MUSTARD IMITATOR	LEWISITE	GAS	GERANIUMS	IRRITATES NASAL PASSAGES. LATER SKIN BURNS, POISON		WASH WITH OIL, HOT WATER, SOAP. CUT AWAY SMALL AREAS OF FLESH 5% SOL'N NA OH, APPLY FERRIC HYDRATE PASTE	OPEN, 1 DAY. WOODS, 1 WEEK WASH DOWN WITH WATER; COVER WITH EARTH. ALCOHOL. NA OH SPRAY
ED	ENEMY'S DELIGHT	ETHYLDICHLORARSINE	GAS	STINGING, LIKE PEPPER IN NOSE	CAUSES SORES, BLISTERS, PARALYSIS OF HANDS		WASH WITH GASOLINE, HOT WATER AND SOAP	ONE HOUR. COVER WITH EARTH. CAUSTIC, NA OH SOLUTION

KEY TO PICTORIAL DIRECTIONS:

MASK PROTECTION NEEDED

FULL PROTECTIVE CLOTHING NEEDED

GENERAL INSTRUCTIONS

THE IMPORTANCE OF PROPER FIRST AID FOR GAS VICTIMS CANNOT BE OVER-EMPHASIZED. THE FOLLOWING ARE GENERAL RULES WHICH APPLY IN ALL CASES.

A. ACT PROMPTLY AND QUIETLY: BE CALM.
B. PUT A GAS MASK ON THE PATIENT IF GAS IS STILL PRESENT OR, IF HE HAS A MASK ON, CHECK TO SEE THAT HIS IS PROPERLY ADJUSTED. IF A MASK IS NOT AVAILABLE, WET A HANDKERCHIEF OR OTHER CLOTH AND HAVE HIM BREATHE THROUGH IT.
C. KEEP THE PATIENT AT ABSOLUTE REST; LOOSEN CLOTHING TO FACILITATE BREATHING.
D. REMOVE THE PATIENT TO A GAS-FREE PLACE AS SOON AS POSSIBLE.
E. SUMMON MEDICAL AID PROMPTLY; IF POSSIBLE, SEND THE VICTIM TO A HOSPITAL.
F. DO NOT PERMIT THE PATIENT TO SMOKE, AS THIS CAUSES COUGHING AND, HENCE, EXERTION.

KEEP THIS CHART! STUDY IT! IT MAY SAVE YOUR LIFE!

Despite the Geneva Protocol that forbade it, the use of chemical and biological weapons was still a threat in World War II. From a 1943 issue of *The Hangar*. (*Courtesy Aroostook County Historical and Art Museum*)

Above left: A Royal Air Force Avro Lancaster heavy bomber on the tarmac. This and following images of planes on the flightline are from the Jules Arel Collection and were not authorized for public release at the time they were created due to the top-secret nature of base activities. (*Courtesy the Cary Library*)

Above right: A pilot poses in front of his Fairey Battle. The Battle was a light-bomber with a crew contingent of three. It had a powerful Rolls-Royce engine and between 1937 and 1940, the Fairey Aviation Company built over 2,000 of these planes. (*Image from the Jules Arel Collection, courtesy of the Cary Library*)

The de Havilland Mosquito was a wood-framed plane and one of the fastest operational aircraft in the world. (*Image from the Jules Arel Collection, courtesy of the Cary Library*)

This American SBD Dauntless was a United States' dive-bomber/scout plane. Thousands of these aircraft were produced by the Northrop Corporation for use during World War II. (*Image from the Jules Arel Collection, courtesy of the Cary Library*)

Grumman G-21 Goose, an amphibious flying boat which was used by Canadian, English, and U.S. armed forces for reconnaissance, transport, rescue, and training. (*Image from the Jules Arel Collection, courtesy of the Cary Library*)

The .50-caliber tail gun of a B-17 Flying Fortress. During missions, the gunner would be in a semi-seated, semi-kneeling position wearing an oxygen mask and a heated fleece-lined suit. There was no room for the gunner to wear his parachute, so it was kept within reach. During training, the gunner was required to field strip the gun while blindfolded and wearing gloves. (*Image from the Jules Arel Collection, courtesy of the Cary Library*)

A B-17 Flying Fortress heavy bomber being serviced by U.S. Army personnel on the Houlton AAF flightline. Between 1936 and 1945, nearly 13,000 of these Flying Fortresses were produced and the aircraft dropped more bombs on Europe during the war than any other Allied aircraft. (*Image from the Jules Arel Collection, courtesy of the Cary Library*)

Above left: A 1943 aerial image of Houlton Army Airfield. (*From the collection of Jules Arel, image courtesy of the Cary Library*)

Above right: The control tower is one of the few remaining structures that is still standing today. This tower saw more than 3,000 aircraft pass through the base during its active use.

This structure is the parachute building and is the only original wooden structure left standing from the air base. Parachute buildings were used to pack, inspect, and store parachutes used by paratroopers and other flight personnel.

Even though new siding and some upgrades have been done to the hangar to keep it functional, the architecture and design are unmistakably of military origin. There were two original hangars from the Army Air Force Base, but unfortunately one was destroyed by fire in 2023.

Inside the last remaining hangar, which still has all the original interior framework. The boiler is no longer functional, and the electricity has been modernized, but walking inside of the spacious hangar is like stepping back in time.

5
COASTAL ARTILLERY

The granite forts and smoothbore cannons of both the Second and Third System fortifications were outpaced quickly during the latter part of the nineteenth century. To meet the defense requirements that made existing fortifications obsolete, the U.S. Government created the Endicott Board in 1885 which would upgrade coastal defense fortifications and weaponry. Endicott system weapons including disappearing rifled-bore guns, mortars, underwater minefields, and submarine nets.[1]

Fortifications were made of iron reinforced concrete, steel, and because of the improved range of the modern guns, special attention was given to observational height and visibility of gun batteries. Artillery batteries were constructed that were made of concrete and designed so that neither the gun nor the fortification would be visible from the water.

In Maine, many existing coastal positions were reimagined or modified, and in other locations, new positions were established. The protection of Portland and Casco Bay saw perhaps some of the most significant changes as it went through substantial defensive development:

> Fort Preble was equipped with mortar batteries as well as new 3" and 6" guns, and entirely new installations were erected on Cow Island (Fort Lyon), Great Diamond Island (Fort Mckinley), Cushing Island (Fort Levett), and Portland Head (Fort Williams). Because Fort Gorges and Fort Scammell could not be redesigned, given their cramped geographical settings, they were converted into storage facilities.[2]

Further up the coast, Fort Baldwin was constructed beginning in 1905 and located on Sabino Head in Phippsburg. The gun batteries were located on the top of Sabino Hill overlooking Fort Popham. Fort Baldwin had a full complement of personal and facilities along with three batteries consisting of two 3-inch guns, one 6-inch disappearing gun, and two 6-inch pedestal guns in their respective batteries.

Fort Baldwin was active throughout World War I and two companies consisting of about 100 personnel were stationed there. As World War I wore on, the threat of a coastal attack on the U.S. became diminished, and the disappearing gun was sent to France. After World War I, Fort Baldwin was decommissioned, and the U.S. Army removed the guns that remained at the fort.[3]

Although it seemed Fort Baldwin was no longer active, construction at the top of Sabino Hill was not finished, and around 1942, when the United States found itself once again involved in a world at war, select locations on the Maine coast began to see towers being built at elevations that offered unobstructed views of the open Atlantic Ocean.

At Fort Baldwin and other key areas, observation towers were constructed that served as fire control towers where observers would call in the precise location of approaching enemy ships to the nearby gun batteries located at Casco Bay; exact positions would be triangulated between control towers. Although Fort Baldwin had been previously disarmed, towed 155-mm M1918 guns were brought in to defend the fort, and from 1942 until January 17, 1944, Battery D, 8th Coast Artillery, protected the fort and manned the fire tower.

During World War II, Casco Bay played a significant role in the six-year campaign that came to be known as the Battle of the Atlantic. The bay served as an important staging area for ships preparing to cross the North Atlantic on their way to Europe as Allied forces kept essential supplies and troops moving to support the war effort. Keeping the shipping lanes open and protecting the supply chain was of paramount concern to American and Allied forces.

Forts and batteries were built or refitted around Portland Harbor, adding 6-inch, 12-inch, and 16-inch guns, and in addition, mortars and extensive networks of searchlights, electronically detonated mines and submarine nets were all created to close off Casco Bay from an enemy incursion.

Built in 1901 and used throughout both the Spanish-American War and World War I, Fort McKinley was the Army headquarters for the defense of Portland Harbor from 1940 until the end of World War II. Typically staffed with 800 troops, the personnel at Fort McKinley swelled to 1,400 during the war as personnel manned nine batteries consisting of twenty-six total guns.[4]

Fort McKinley was abandoned by the U.S. Army in 1947, and for nearly forty years, it fell into disrepair before the fort area was purchased, developed, and placed on the National Register of Historic Places. Today, most all batteries at all forts have become derelict, and at some locations only remnants remain, but Fort McKinley's fort area is well preserved and is now maintained as a private gated community.

Opposite above: A 12-inch M1895 gun being fired from its coastal defensive position. Location and date unknown.[5]

Opposite below left: Fire control tower at Two Lights State Park in Cape Elizabeth. This tower was built next to a farmhouse and was designed to resemble a silo to avoid detection. Ironically, the farmhouse burned down shortly after construction of the tower was complete. This tower coordinated with the tower at Fort Baldwin to triangulate offshore enemy positions.

Opposite below right: The fire control tower at Fort Baldwin. This five-story monolithic structure has been watching over the mouth of the Kennebec River for more than eighty years.

An aerial photograph of Fort Popham with the gun batteries of Fort Baldwin barely visible on the hill behind it, *c.* 1936.[6]

Battery Cogan, Fort Baldwin. Now obscured by trees, the batteries at Fort Baldwin once had an unobstructed view of the waters below. This battery was named for Patrick Cogan who was a lieutenant during the Revolutionary War. Battery Cogan had two 3-inch M1903 guns.

The 6-inch disappearing gun was positioned here before it was shipped to France during World War I. This battery was named for John Hardman, a captain during the Revolutionary War who was captured in 1780 and died while he was a prisoner of war.

Although the exteriors of each battery look very utilitarian and sensible, the personnel quarters of the battery interiors were designed with a bit more comfort and visual appeal.

This once-classified 1936 aerial image of Fort McKinley on Great Diamond Island offers a good view of the parade grounds surrounded by personnel living quarters.[7]

A 2024 image of the parade grounds. The barracks buildings and officers' quarters are all in immaculate condition and maintained as private residences on the island. Developers must adhere to strict codes put forth by the community and structures must be restored and maintained at near original condition.

One side of the parade grounds had barracks buildings for enlisted personnel and on the other side there were duplexes that each housed two officers. Today, they are all used as private residences.

One of the few buildings that remains in a state of entropy. The Army hospital at Fort McKinley is in the process of being acquired and developed, but community building restrictions make it a slow and costly endeavor.

This postcard from Fort Mckinley when it was an active fort depicts the hospital in much better condition than it is in today.[8]

A fire control observation post in the battery area at Fort McKinley. This post once had an unobstructed view of the open Atlantic Ocean, but it has since become grown in and heavily forested.

6
NAVAL SECURITY GROUP ACTIVITY (NSGA) WINTER HARBOR

The NSGA began with a radio enthusiast who turned into a patriotic landowner wanting to do his part at the onset of World War I. Alessandro Fabbri recognized that his parcel of land at Mount Dessert Island's Otter Cliffs, with its unobstructed view of the open Atlantic Ocean, would make a perfect location for a radio station. Taking the initiative, he built and equipped a station on his own. In exchange for a command and commission, Fabbri transferred ownership of the land to the U.S. Navy to be utilized as a naval radio station and the station was commissioned on August 28, 1917, with Ensign Alessandro Fabbri in command.

The radio station functioned throughout the war and continued for many years after, but by 1933 the buildings were becoming run-down and dilapidated. In the interest of expanding Acadia National Park, philanthropist John D. Rockefeller Jr. lobbied to have the station removed but was met with resistance from the U.S. Navy who had come to view the station as one of the most important radio stations on the east coast. The station was able to receive radio traffic from Europe, Iceland, and Newfoundland when atmospheric conditions prevented other East Coast stations from receiving any signal.[1]

In a compromise between Rockefeller, the National Park Service (NPS), and the U.S. Navy, a location in Winter Harbor was ultimately selected for a new radio station. Located at the end of the Schoodic Peninsula on Big Moose Island (about 5 miles across Frenchman's Bay from the Otter Cliffs station) a new station was built. Among the structures constructed for the new station, the most notable was a large apartment building for personnel and radio operations. The large stonework building was similar in appearance to that of Rockefeller's summer residence in Seal Harbor.[2]

By 1935, Winter Harbor was among eleven sites chosen for a newly developed high-frequency direction finding technology and the U.S. Navy Radio and Direction-Finding Station, Winter Harbor, was commissioned on February 28, 1935.

Toward the end of World War II and into the Cold War, security activities at the station increased and the base expanded, adding an additional 152 acres in 1947. In 1950, the station was redesignated U.S Naval Security Group Detachment, U.S. Naval Radio Station, Winter Harbor, Maine.

As the Cold War intensified, so did the expansion and activities at the station and additional sites were added on nearby Corea, located on a peninsula just east of the

Schoodic Peninsula. With this expansion, the station was redesignated as the Naval Security Group Activity, Winter Harbor.[3]

In 1962, a large high-frequency antenna array (HFDF) was constructed at the Corea location and all communications operations were moved there. The Winter Harbor site was then used for administration, housing, and recreation by naval personnel.

In 2001, the U.S. Navy announced the closure of the base, and in March 2002, NSGA Winter Harbor was disestablished by the U.S. Navy.[4] In July 2002, the Winter Harbor property was transferred to the National Park Service as part of Acadia National Park.

The Corea site is now largely abandoned and dilapidated and land surrounding the area of the Corea station is being managed by the U.S. Fish and Wildlife Service as a National Wildlife Refuge.

Operating force personnel posing on an antenna at Otter Cliffs Naval Radio Station, Mount Desert Island, March 6, 1919. Alessandro Fabbri is standing at center, front row.[5]

U.S. Navy Radio and Direction-Finding Station, Winter Harbor. The apartment building sits between two 210-foot radio towers which were raised in the fall of 1933. There were seven structures in the original station complex, including the three in this image.[6]

The eleven-unit apartment building designed by New York architect Grosvenor Atterbury and constructed in French Eclectic Revival style. The building was built for housing and radio operations. This is facing southeast, looking at the rear of the building.[7]

The same perspective as the previous image, but with a wider view of the entire building, garage doors and a partial view of the attached powerhouse to the right. The building is now named Rockefeller Hall, and it is used as an education center and park operations building for Acadia National Park. (2024 photo.)

Rockefeller Hall, and the powerhouse to the left. The plaque on the anchor reads, "Dedicated to the officer, enlisted and civilian personnel who served with the United States Navy at Naval Security Group Activity Winter Harbor. 1935–2002."

Left: A satellite view of the Corea station. The circular HFDF array dwarfs the other structures at the station.[8]

Below: In the late 1960s-early 1970s, satellite communication was integrated into naval detection systems. The advanced tactical Ocean surveillance system or "Classic Wizard" incorporated ground-based radomes that triangulated with corresponding surveillance satellites. These were used in the detection of Soviet naval activity during the Cold War.[9]

The elephant cage, AKA Wullenweber antenna, was an AN/FRD-10 circularly disposed antenna array used in high-frequency direction finding. Radio signals could be triangulated using this system for the purpose of navigation, intelligence gathering, search and rescue, and law enforcement. The array was so large, local fishermen would use it to aid in their visual navigation of the area.[10]

A 2024 aerial view of the Corea station. The operations building for the Classic Wizard system is in the foreground and the base platforms of the small radome arrays are barely visible in the trees starting at the right upper-hand corner of the building. Slightly to the left in the image background, the circular formation of the trees indicates the location of the elephant cage which was removed in 2009.

The Corea location resembles that of a post-apocalyptic world. Vandalism, graffiti, and entropy are prominent in the area and very little remains of the order, security and organization that was once present at NSGA Winter Harbor.

Above left: The Corea station has suffered many years of neglect, and the interior spaces now only vaguely resemble what was once a highly classified communications and radio interception station.

Above right: After exploring all the spaces of the once-secure base, this is the only evidence I was able to find that indicated the past presence of the U.S. Navy.

7
THE COLD WAR

The bombing of the Japanese cities of Nagasaki and Hiroshima ushered in the atomic age of modern warfare and demonstrated to the world the sheer destructive power of the atomic bomb. With these bombings, World War II came to an end and a new kind of war began. A war that didn't involve tanks, foxholes, or troops on the ground, but instead it involved the threat of nuclear annihilation from the skies.

The Soviet Union, led by Russia (who had been an ally during the war), emerged from World War II as a superpower and controlling member of the Eastern Bloc. Joseph Stalin and his newly expanded nation then began a tense ideological clash with the United States and its western allies. As the Soviets developed their own atomic weapons technology, an arms race began as the United States and Russia struggled for world dominance. The threat of nuclear annihilation seemingly became the only deterrent preventing an all-out nuclear war.

It was the age of the Cold War, a war that never was, which lasted four decades. The Cold War era created a worldwide existential fear of nuclear holocaust and cost billions of dollars in infrastructure buildup; much of which has been left behind, written off, or discarded. Entire bases were constructed for heavy bombers armed with nuclear weapons, as were radar stations, missile launch facilities, and nuclear weapons storage areas. Thousands of personnel were stationed at these locations where twenty-four hours a day, seven days a week, they actively prepared for nuclear war.

Although many parts of the state saw a buildup of military infrastructure during this period, none was as profound as the buildup which took place in Aroostook County. After the creation of the United States Air Force in 1947, the newly formed branch of U.S. military built a long-range heavy bomber base in Limestone that was the most heavily armed Strategic Air Command base in the United States.

In *The Aroostook Arms Race: Cold War in the Crown of Maine*, I highlight the transitions that took place in this rural area of Maine and explain how a sparsely populated county in northern Maine became a hub for transient nuclear-armed aircraft and a heavily armed defensive stronghold for the United States during the Cold War. This chapter is but a glimpse into the activities that took place during the Cold War in northern Maine. A more thorough discussion of this era and its impact on Aroostook County are detailed in my book.

Weapons storage bunkers (or igloos) in Limestone that were once part of the top-secret Caribou Air Force Station—the largest operational nuclear weapons storage facility in the United States.

The arch hangar of Loring Air Force Base—a first-generation maintenance hangar for the B-36 bomber. It was built in 1948 and was one of the first structures to be built for Strategic Air Command. Today, it is one of only two such hangars in the world.

Nike site L-13, Caswell—a U.S. Army Anti-Aircraft Command Nike missile launch facility—was one of four Nike missile bases that was active in Aroostook County. This was also one of two missile sites equipped with the nuclear-capable Nike Hercules missile.

A nuclear Snark missile being offloaded from a transport plane at Presque Isle AFB. The Snark missile base at Presque Isle was active during the third and final time the base was used by the military. Presque Isle was an army airfield from 1941–1945, an ADC fighter-interceptor base from 1948–1959, and, finally, a SAC AFB (ICM-Snark) from 1959–1961. (*Oscar "Voscar" Nelder Photo. Reproduced from the collection of Dr. Graves, used by permission*)

8
DOW AAF, AFB, AND BOMARC MISSILE SITE

Before becoming a Strategic Air Command heavy bomber base during the Cold War, Dow went through many transitions beginning in 1923 when General "Billy" Mitchell landed a fleet of twenty-six Martin bombers and de Havilland scout planes on the Rich Farm in Bangor. At the time, General Mitchell's fleet constituted the entire Air Force of the United States, and after arriving, the visiting general went on to tell Bangor Rotarians that he envisioned a great future in military aviation for Bangor. The Rich Farm was located on property that would become Dow Army Airfield, but it would not come to be recognized as such until 1940, after nearly twenty years of development as a municipal airport for the City of Bangor.[1]

On July 12, 1940, the U.S. Army listed the site as a primary location for an aerial defense airfield based in Maine. Bangor was seen as an ideal defensive position against an enemy incursion from Europe and the city immediately began upgrading the airfield for the defense mission. Then in September, the Air Defense Survey Board recommended that a heavy bombardment group be stationed at Bangor.

The U.S. Army Corp of Engineers began to work on construction of the U.S. Army airfield with Congress' authorization. Special considerations had to be accounted for due to the significant winters in Maine and the weight of the new heavy super bombers which weighed nearly 140,000 pounds each. Work progressed quickly and by 1941, the U.S. Army Air Force's 43rd Bombardment Group was training at the newly created airfield with B-17 Flying Fortresses.

In January 1942, the U.S. Army airfield at Bangor was renamed Dow Field in honor of 2nd Lt. James Frederick Dow of Oakland who was killed in a crash involving two bombers over Queensborough, New York, in 1940.

Also in 1942, the 43rd transferred its operations to the Pacific Theater, and with the departure of the 43rd, the mission of Dow Army Airfield changed significantly. Bangor's location was ideal for transient air traffic bound for Europe via the North Atlantic, and Dow was designated as a transfer point for Army Air Transport Command (ATC), North Atlantic Transport Route; control of the Dow Airfield was transferred to Air Transport Command's North Atlantic Division, headquartered at the Presque Isle Army Airfield.

ATC began using Dow as a significant hub and by the spring of 1943 "kept a steady flow of B-24's and B-17's moving eastward across the Atlantic."[2] Transport planes, fighters, and tactical bombers all made their way through Dow during its time as a North Atlantic ferrying base. Before continuing across the North Atlantic, or upon arriving from European missions, flight crews were billeted, fed, given medical care, and briefed at Dow. In addition to the obvious tactical support that the bombers provided in Europe, they also played a significant secondary role for troops when all available space in the large Europe-bound bombers was packed with mail destined for deployed personnel overseas.

In addition to hosting training facilities and its role as a ferrying, staging, and support base, Dow also played a role in the Battle of the Atlantic. Beginning in 1942, the USAAF's 92nd Reconnaissance Group flew coordinated anti-submarine patrols from Dow AAF using Lockheed A-29 Hudson aircraft.

During World War II, upwards of 100,000 combat personnel traveled through Dow going to or coming from Europe. Activities at Dow peaked in July 1944 when over 700 combat aircraft processed through the base during the one month alone. Nearly 6,500 aircraft passed through Dow during World War II, and at its height, 7,000 personnel were stationed there.[3] After the war, activities at Dow AAF dropped drastically and except for the Air National Guard, the military presence at Bangor nearly vanished.

After a period of inactivity, the newly formed U.S. Air Force took control of the base, renaming it Dow Air Force Base and then deactivating it again, all in 1947. Four years later, on February 1, 1951, events in Korea led to the U.S. Air Force reactivating many bases, Dow being among them. At first, command was under Air Defense Command (ADC), with SAC taking over control of the base in April of the same year.

More command structure changes took place in 1952 when the base was transferred from SAC to Tactical Air Command (TAC), and then back to SAC, all within a six-month period. The base finally came under the final control of SAC in September 1954, and shortly thereafter, massive restructuring and redevelopment began to modernize old facilities and bring the base up to date for modern heavy jet aircraft. Between 1954 and 1957, a new single runway was installed, and an alert area and parking apron were added. In addition, new hangars, a fighter alert facility, administrative buildings, and air police facilities were all added, as well as upgrades to the weapons storage area.

Weapons stored on Dow AFB consisted of a variety of conventional and nuclear munitions, including Hound Dog missiles, which were B-52-mounted cruise missiles armed with W28 thermonuclear warheads. The warheads could be preset to yield a range from 70 kilotons to 1.45 megatons.

Additionally, a storage area was added for the air defense mission which could store around 150 MB-1 Genie air-to-air missiles. The missiles could travel at Mach 3 with a range of 6 miles. The weapons were tipped with a W25 nuclear warhead that could deliver a 1.5 kiloton punch to their targets.[4]

Dow AFB hosted the largest storage facility for these missiles on the east coast and the facility "stored more air defense weapons than any site located in the northeast."[5] One of the largest nuclear storage areas for ADC was in Bangor, a mere 173 miles from Limestone, the location of SAC's largest operational nuclear storage facility.

In the early to mid-1960s, defending Dow was not done by fighter jets alone. From June 1, 1959, to December 15, 1964, the ADC's 30th Air Defense Missile Squadron watched the skies from the BOMARC missile base located less than 4 miles from Dow AFB. The CIM-10 BOMARC missile was a surface-to-air interceptor missile which could travel at Mach 2.8, had a max range of more than 200 miles, and a cruising altitude of 65,000 feet. This nuclear capable missile could be armed with a W40 10-kiloton nuclear warhead.[6]

The Bangor BOMARC facility achieved operational readiness on December 12, 1960, and the site was the first to achieve operational readiness within the BOMARC program. The missile site had its own power and HVAC plant, administrative buildings, a missile maintenance building and twenty-eight missile silos, nicknamed coffin silos, which were structures that the missiles would be stored in horizontally. The weapons could be raised to a vertical firing position within seconds, launching the 47-foot-long, 15,000-pound missile at its target. The BOMARC relied on both the SAGE radar network (discussed in Chapter 13) and nearby Dow AFB for logistical support.

Missiles, rockets, bombers, fighters, an award-winning refueling squadron, and more were at Dow or flew through Dow at one time or another between 1954 and 1968 (when Dow AFB was closed for good). The area is now occupied by the Bangor Air National Guard, which still has an award-winning refueling squadron; the 101st Air Refueling Wing is one of the most decorated Air National Guard units in the United States.

B-24 Liberator bombers on the tarmac during World War II. The bomb symbols and swastikas painted underneath the cockpit provide visual evidence of the aircraft's previous successful European missions. (*Image Courtesy of Maine Aviation Museum*)

Photograph of the newly constructed SAC control tower, Dow AFB, July 27, 1956.[7]

The north–south runway under construction in 1957. The massive 11,400-foot-long runway was a drastic change from the U.S. Army's three runway design. Still to this day, the runway represents major engineering accomplishments for both the U.S. Air Force and the City of Bangor.[8]

A B-52 stands ready on the parking ramp with the control tower and an emergency response truck in the background.[9]

A 1996 aerial image of Bangor International Airport which utilizes the runway created by the U.S. Air Force. Despite this photo being taken twenty-eight years after the departure of SAC, the two alert aprons (aka Christmas Trees) remain very prominent in the bottom right-hand corner. The aprons were used to park alert-aircraft which maintained a constant state of nuclear readiness while crews waited in the adjoining underground alert area or "molehole."[10]

Construction of the ADC weapons storage facility for the MB-1 Genie missile, August 17, 1959. The concrete units being built resemble modern self-storage units that are familiar to most everyone.[11]

A 2024 image of the Genie missile storage units which are now being used as a modern self-storage facility.

This earth-covered weapons storage structure once housed the Genie W25 nuclear warheads which weighed 220 lbs., were 26 inches long, and had a blast yield of 1.7 kilotons.

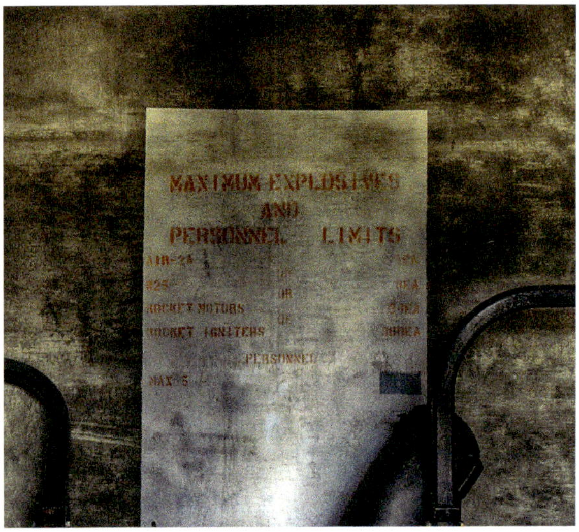

Left: According to the notice painted on the wall, the storage of W25 nuclear warheads in this unit was limited to eight warheads.

Below: A May 7, 1963, satellite view of the BOMARC missile facility in Bangor. The neatly spaced rows of the coffin silos are easy to discern.[12]

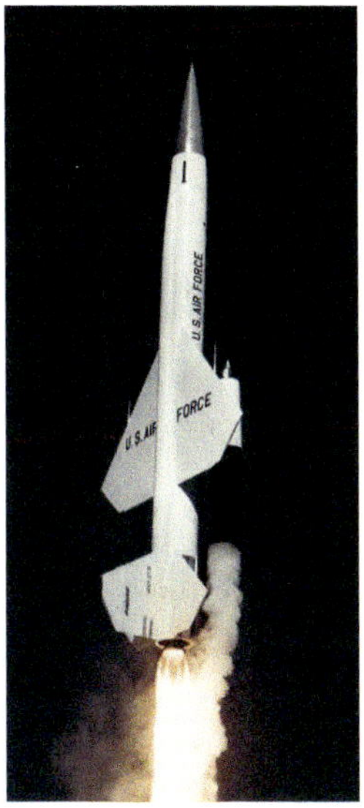

Above left: A Boeing IM-99 BOMARC interceptor missile being launched from the Cape Canaveral test annex, December 13, 1958.[13]

Above right: BOMARC missiles after being raised from the storage silos and locked into firing positions.[14]

A 2024 aerial image showing a partial view of the BOMARC facility. Note the structures in the foreground, these were once the missile silos which have been converted to accommodate small businesses.

The original heating and power building remains standing and still resembles its original appearance. Local businesses now operate from the remaining structures at the missile site location.

A considerable amount of modernization and upgrades have been done to the building that was once the missile assembly plant and maintenance building.

9
AN EYE TO THE SKIES

Air Defense Command (ADC) was not just fighter jets, missiles, and rockets. The advancing enemy could not be intercepted if it were not first detected, and detection was an important part of the early development of ADC. At first, Lash-Up radar was used in both the Bangor (Dow) and Limestone (Loring) Air Defense Sectors. The Lash-Up sites were temporary and active in the late 1940s and early 1950s.

The term Lash-Up was derived from its literal meaning when World War II surplus radars were somewhat hastily "lashed" together on wooden platforms or quickly erected towers to create the radar network. In 1948, a plan was announced to replace Lash-Up sites and put in seventy-five permanent radar stations in the United States and Canada, but the plans met with budgeting restrictions. Public support would wax and wane as world events (such as Russia detonating an atomic bomb) would temporarily invigorate the public, but it was not until December 1949 when the first twenty-four of the sites were scheduled to be built.

As the permanent radar stations became viable, it was surmised that the system which was in place would only be effective at curtailing 30 percent of an enemy bomber incursion. To address this unacceptable number, a defense lab was ultimately set up at the Massachusetts Institute of Technology (MIT) and named Lincoln Laboratory. The Lincoln Laboratory immediately began working on a computer that could network all radar stations together using telephone lines. The controlling computer (named the Whirlwind) was a supercomputer which would take years of testing and development before being ready to be placed online.[1]

On April 16, 1952, sites in Maine and Alaska received reports of unidentified inbound aircraft which caused hundreds of intercept aircraft to be scrambled in anticipation of an approaching enemy. It was soon realized that it was a false alarm, but with it came a new sense of urgency in the accuracy and placement of radars. In addition to ongoing developments and plans, it was also decided that a 3,000-mile-long Distant Early Warning (DEW) line needed to be established in northernmost Canada, Alaska, and Greenland. This was in addition to the Pine Tree Line which ran along the border of the United States and Canada. By late 1952, permanent systems were largely in place with plans to build more and establish a more complete network.[2]

Permanent system radar stations replaced Lash-Up systems in the two Maine defense sectors, and as the name implies, the new stations were constructed with permanency in mind. Brunswick Air Force Station was the first out of twenty-four stations during the first phase of development, and despite its status as a permanent station, it was the first of such stations in Maine to close.

Aside from Brunswick AFS, locations for permanent system stations were also selected in Charleston, Caswell, and Bucks Harbor and they were constructed in that order, with Charleston and Caswell being built at nearly the same time.

All the stations functioned as ground-control intercept (GCI) stations, manually guiding interceptor aircraft toward intruding enemy aircraft detected on station radar arrays which consisted of search radars and height-finder radars. In 1958–1959, all the radar stations became part of the SAGE network which incorporated the new supercomputer (discussed in Chapter 13).

10
BRUNSWICK AIR FORCE STATION

During phase one development of the ADC's permanent radar network, Brunswick Air Force Station was activated in 1951. Manned by the 654th Aircraft Control and Warning Squadron, the station served as a manual ground-intercept and warning station until 1955 when it became part of the early SAGE network, jointly sharing data with other radar bases in the network.

The early SAGE network began with just a handful of locations while the "bugs" were worked out of the system as it developed into a viable network of radars feeding data into a control center. Brunswick AFS was part of the initial experimental network, feeding data to the Whirlwind I computer located in Cambridge, Massachusetts. The early network is best summed up by MIT:

> Lincoln Laboratory started to set up an experimental system and named it, for its location, the Cape Cod System. It was functionally complete; all air defense functions could be demonstrated, tested, and modified. The Cape Cod System was a model air defense system, scaled down in size but realistically embodying all operational functions.[1]

Brunswick was part of the Cape Cod System until the SAGE system expanded and Topsham Air Force Station was opened as a SAGE direction center; Brunswick then became part of the regional SAGE network. After joining the SAGE network, the 654th AC&W Squadron was redesignated the 654th Radar Squadron.[2]

During a consolidation of ADC resources, the base was deactivated in 1965. After deactivation, one of the radars was sent to nearby Topsham Air Force Station and the remainder of the facility was acquired by the U.S. Navy and absorbed into the Brunswick Naval Air Station.

During its use by the U.S. Navy, the station location became the Anti-Submarine Classification and Analysis Center (ASCAC) which worked in conjunction with airborne aircraft to locate and identify oceangoing submarines.

All that remains of the Brunswick AFS is a single radar tower that has been modified and repurposed. Security fencing remains in place and the area remains a high security area. Rather than a secure military facility, it is now a secure civilian data facility.

11
CHARLESTON AFS & CASWELL AFS

Charleston is approximately 28 miles northwest of Bangor and construction began on the Charleston Air Force Station at the top of Bull Hill in 1950. In early 1951, the station was manned, and by June 1952, the station was fully operational. The station was manned by the 765th Aircraft Control and Warning Squadron which later became the 765th Radar Squadron (SAGE) in 1959.

The 765th operated the station as an Air Defense Direction Center with a manual capability from 1952 until 1959. From 1959, the station operated under the Bangor Air Defense sector providing search and height data to the SAGE network. The station also provided ground to air communications and aircraft control as a Back-up Interceptor Control (BUIC) area, and the station offered support in the detection and warning of sea-launched ballistic missiles.[1]

The station was closed, and the squadron deactivated in 1979. Most of the property is now under the control of the State of Maine Department of Corrections.[2]

Similar to Charleston AFS which replaced the Lash-Up radar at Dow, Caswell Air Force Station replaced the Lash-Up radar at Limestone (Loring). The Caswell AFS was an Aircraft Control and Warning Station for the Limestone Air Defense Sector which became operational in 1951. The 766th Radar Squadron (formally 766 Aircraft Control and Warning Squadron) was assigned to the base, and in 1959, the station joined the SAGE network and began feeding data to Topsham AFS.

In 1980, the station was deactivated, not long before ADC's deactivation.[3]

Construction of an AN/FPS-27 radar tower, June 13, 1961. The Charleston AFS was the first station in the United States to receive the long-range AN/FPS-27 search radar in 1963.[4]

The ominous clouds of a January sky add some apocalyptic-like drama to the abandoned base. The tall blue tower was once the AN/FPS 27 search radar, and on the right, a height-finder radar base.

An abandoned utility truck sits behind the BUIC blockhouse. A height finder radar base is in the left background.

AN FPS-6 height finder tower which may have also held an earlier search finder radar.

This structure was for an AN/FPS-26 which later converted to an AN-FSS-7 to aid in the surveillance of potential missiles launched from Soviet ballistic missile submarines.

An aerial view of the five remaining towers. The radar operations building is in the center with the BUIC blockhouse.

Right: The rusted door leading into a radar tower still displays the Air Force Communications Services emblem.

Below: A 2024 image of the Caswell AFS location. Some evidence of the U.S. Air Force remains but the property is now privately owned by a local potato grower whose fields surround the station property (which is now used for farm operations).

12
BUCKS HARBOR AFS, 1955–1979

The radar station at Bucks Harbor was originally planned to be constructed on the peninsula of Corea, but the U.S. Navy feared that a radar station would interfere with its nearby radio station, so in the town of Machiasport on the Bold Coast of Maine, Bucks Harbor was selected for the location of the distant early-warning station; Bucks Harbor Air Force Station was activated in 1955.

The site was originally designated to protect the Loring Defense Area and initially served as a GCI and warning station. The 907th AC&W Squadron watched the skies for approaching enemy aircraft to guide interceptor aircraft to any inbound intruders detected.

In 1959, the squadron was redesignated the 907th Radar Squadron (SAGE) when it joined the SAGE network and began feeding data to the SAGE network.[1]

The Bucks Harbor AFS was deactivated in 1979 and most of the property was purchased by the State of Maine. The Federal Aviation Administration (FAA) still operates Joint Air Route Surveillance radar from the site and is part of the North American Aerospace Defense Command (NORAD) Eastern Air Defense Sector; Maine also has a Department of Corrections facility on the property.

Bucks Harbor AFS during its active use, *c.* 1966. The station and radar arrays sit on top of the hill and base housing is in the valley below. In 1965, the station became a joint use facility, and the FAA began operations from the station as well.[2]

One of the most impressive features of the Bucks Harbor area is the crescent-shaped shoreline known as Jasper Beach; the public beach is approximately a half-mile long and features millions of polished cobblestone pebbles comprised of volcanic stones, primarily rhyolite (which resembles Jasper) that have been polished by the surf for eons.[3]

U.S. Air Force remnants can still be found in various places throughout the AFS location, but the modern world is quickly taking over.

The housing complex sits abandoned; attempts to repurpose the area have resulted in the discovery of over eleven chemicals including trichloroethylene (which was once used for cleaning radar equipment) in the water table. The U.S. Army Corp of Engineers are engaged in ongoing efforts to remediate the water supply in the area.[4]

The old and the new; the abandoned base housing complex still sits in the valley and resembles a ghost town as the active ARSR-4 FAA surveillance radar watches over the area from the top of Howard Mountain.

13
SAGE & TOPSHAM AFS

The Semi-Automatic Ground Environment (SAGE) was a defense radar network and the brainchild of Lincoln Laboratory at MIT. If radars in the network were to detect approaching enemy aircraft, radar data would be sent to the nearest SAGE direction center via phone lines. Once the data was received, continuous targeting information would be sent out to the intercept (combat) stations best located to neutralize the threat. The SAGE network was developed between 1948 and 1958 with a price tag of nearly $10 billion (three times the cost of the Manhattan Project) for its decade of development.[1]

By 1962, the SAGE system was completed, comprising 142 primary radar stations, ninety-six gap filler sites, and offshore Texas Towers. Radar stations were situated throughout the United States, Canada, Greenland, and Iceland. The entire defense network consisted of more than forty interceptor squadrons, numbering approximately 800 aircraft, seven BOMARC missile battalions, and scores of army NIKE missile battalions all networked into the SAGE system.

The network would not have been possible if it weren't for the Whirlwind II computer which began development in 1952 from the first-generation Whirlwind computer. Designed by Lincoln Laboratory and built by both Lincoln Laboratory and IBM, the prototype computer went online in 1955 (redesignated the AN/FSQ-7) as an integral part of the Cape Cod System. This beast of a computer weighed an astonishing 250 tons, contained 49,000 vacuum tubes, and had a 3,000-kilowatt power supply.

Creating the first computer network would not have been possible without its software, and in the words of Lincoln Laboratory, "the software task developed quickly into the largest real-time control program ever coded, and all the coding had to be done in machine language since higher-order languages did not yet exist. The art of computer programing was essentially invented for SAGE."[2]

The Topsham Air Force Station was established as a SAGE direction center beginning in 1957. Rather than the host of radars that the other SAGE network stations had, the Topsham AFS featured the large blockhouse as a prominent part of the station. The blockhouse contained "the heart of the SAGE system," the AN/FSQ-7 which processed radar data, sending out location and direction information if inbound targets were detected—all at the speed of sound across phone lines.[3]

For twelve years the direction center operated, and in 1969, advances in the SAGE network allowed for Aerospace Defense Command (redesignated in 1968 from Air

Defense Command) to decrease the number of SAGE direction centers, and the Topsham AFS was deactivated.

After the station closed, the property was taken over by the U.S. Navy who created an annex for the nearby naval air station, creating housing, a commissary, and other outlets. The blockhouse was razed in 1985 and now barely a trace of Topsham AFS remains.

Above: Data from early-warning radar sites would be processed at the station and if a threat would have been perceived, alerts would be activated via Combat Centers to nearby interceptor air bases, missile batteries and NORAD Command.[4]

Below: The Topsham direction center was one of twenty-four in the United States, and each had the telltale blockhouse. Much of the interior inside the four-story blockhouse was taken up by the world's first IBM mainframe computer, the AN/FSQ-7. It was capable of 75,000 instructions per second, and to maintain maximum reliability and connectivity, the system was duplexed, essentially linking two computers which took up nearly a half-acre of floor space.[5] (*Photo by John Stanton*)

14
EXPERIMENTAL SAGE SUBSECTOR, 1955–1962

Before the SAGE network became a viable network, many technical issues had to be worked out of the system, including building the state-of-the-art Whirlwind computer which was used in the initial Cape Cod System.

As the Cape Cod System became functional and expanded its network, it was discovered that the L and S band GCI radars being used were picking up significant amounts of clutter. To try and find a radar that could be added to the network and reduce the clutter, the Experimental SAGE Subsector was created. Jug Handle Hill in West Bath was one of two sites chosen for the experimental SAGE radar testing, the other being in Cape Cod, Massachusetts.

Jug Handle Hill was selected as one of the highest points of mid-coast Maine, and in 1955, testing began with a prototype AN/FPS-31 UHF narrowband search radar. It was the first and only radar of its kind and was so powerful it detected echoes which were created by the region's aurora borealis, commonly referred to as the northern lights. The new experimental radar was so sensitive, it was detecting the phenomenon in the distant north, high up in the atmosphere. Another problem occurred in the early tests when nearby traffic on Route 1 was causing the radar to jam. These problems were subsequently rectified when the transmitter's fixed-tuned magnetron (which generates high-powered pulses used to detect objects) was replaced with an adjustable one.

Both the technical and mechanical problems that were experienced with the radar led to subsequent designs of other early warning tracking radars, and although Bath's FPS-31 was never mass produced, it was considered a success for the development of radars in the SAGE network.[1]

The West Bath location was the primary sensor location for the Experimental SAGE Subsector. As the network grew, new stations were added to the Cape Cod System, and it evolved into the SAGE Network. The MITRE Corporation took over the Experimental SAGE Subsector including the Jug Handle Hill site on July 21, 1958; the site was closed, and the antenna was removed from the tower in November 1962.

The tower was repurposed, and it got more use in the 1970s when the Newcastle-based VAST corporation built a tank into the structure for underwater research and testing by both military and civilian agencies. The U.S. Navy was among those who used the facility testing sonar equipment, and the converted radar tower was used as an oceanographic research and testing facility for nearly two years. In 1974, the U.S. Navy discontinued the testing that they had been conducting, and the complex was closed shortly afterwards.[2]

The property is now in private ownership.

The AN/FPS-31 antenna was 120 feet wide and 16 feet high. The massive boomerang-shaped antenna rotated six times per minute on one large steel bearing (a subsequent design from a previous wheeled carriage system). (*Circa 1956 photo, courtesy The MITRE Corporation*)

During the time of its use in the SAGE network there were also two standard FPS-6 height-finder radars on site. The building in the photo was used as an administrative building to process and transmit radar data. (*Circa 1956 photo, courtesy The MITRE Corporation*)

The tank was able to hold 450,000 gallons of water and a control house was added to the top of the structure as well as a one-ton electric hoist. An auto mechanic now runs a repair business on the property.

Water for the tank was pumped from the small pond that can be seen behind the tower in this aerial photo. The pump and filtration system would allow for the water in the tank to be completely replaced in sixteen hours. The 100-foot-tall tower now has a modern communication antenna on it.

15
GAP-FILLER RADAR

Like the Lash-Up radars, gap-filler radars were literally named. The gap-filler radar filled in the "gaps" in the SAGE network and allowed for more thorough coverage, or in the words of USAF Air Combat command: "Gap-filler radars were designed to cover areas where enemy aircraft could fly low enough to evade detection by distant long-range search radars."[1]

In fact, the gap-fillers worked so well, they allowed for the dissolution of the GOC: "Because the introduction of gap-filler radars alleviated the need for civilians to scan the skies for enemy bombers, the ADC disestablished the Ground Observer Corp on Jan. 31, 1959."[2]

There were three unmanned gap-filler sites in Maine; in Bridgewater, there was a gap-filler for Caswell AFS and the Loring (Limestone) Air Defense Sector, and both Sedgwick and Topsfield had gap-fillers in place for Charleston AFS. Sedgwick was initially monitored by the Brunswick AFS, but after Brunswick's deactivation, it moved to the control of Charleston and the Bangor Air Defense sector.

Changing of the guard

Budd is building advanced, more powerful "gap-filler" radar to replace the radar that now guards low-lying areas of our nation. It will greatly narrow the possibility of an airborne marauder slipping through our defenses. Unmanned, completely automatic stations of the system will feed information to "heavy" radar sites, where high-speed data processing equipment can instantly determine speed, altitude, direction, size and numbers of any invader. Budd is building the new "gap-filler" radar system for the North American Defense Command's SAGE System. It is one of many Budd developments which add new muscle to our nation's defenses. Our Electronics Division offers unique career opportunities for scientists and engineers in this field. For information, write The Budd Company, Phila. 32, Pa.

In electronics, plastics and metals,
Budd works to make tomorrow... today

THE Budd COMPANY
OFFICES AND PLANTS IN PRINCIPAL CITIES

A magazine advertisement from 1962 for the Budd Company which was busy building gap-filler radars (typically AN/FPS-14 and AN/FPS-18 medium-range search radars) to keep the nation safe.[3]

The Topsfield gap-filler site and its generator room, which is attached to a larger equipment room and is not visible through the trees.

The Topsfield gap-filler radar tower doubled as a fire control tower at the top of Musquash Mountain and had an AN/FPS-18 medium-range search radar mounted on it. Modern cellular phone and communications towers now surround the structure.

16
BRUNSWICK NAVAL AIR STATION

Built in 1935 as part of the United States' New Deal Program, the Brunswick airfield operated as a commercial airfield until 1943 when it was taken over and commissioned by the U.S. Navy as Brunswick Naval Air Station.

Beginning in November 1943, Brunswick NAS served as a training base for British Royal Navy Fleet Air Arm squadrons. These squadrons conducted training with Grumman Avenger, Grumman Hellcat, and Vought Corsair aircraft, utilizing the 1,480-acre airfield as well as other satellite airfields located in Maine (such as a USN Auxiliary Airfield Bar Harbor, located in Trenton). In addition to training, British aviators also assisted U.S Navy pilots conducting maritime submarine patrols.[1]

Early in the war, conventional ground warfare had been quickly overshadowed by maritime warfare. The threat of German U-boat attacks became an extremely grave concern to the Allied war effort as German U-boat groups, known as Wolf-Packs, would hunt and maliciously attack merchant vessels and supply ships without provocation, sinking thousands of vessels in the early years of the war. British Prime Minister Winston Churchill famously said, "the only thing that ever really frightened me during the war was the U-boat peril," and it wasn't until 1943 when the United States and Allied forces developed advanced methods to detect and neutralize the threat; by the end of 1943, the German losses began to exceed their ability to counteract them, and it was a turning point in the campaign for the Atlantic shipping lanes.

As the war progressed, the U.S. Navy perfected many methods of detecting and eliminating the threat of enemy submarines, not the least of which being airborne maritime patrols. The first U.S. patrol squadron to be assigned to Brunswick NAS was the heavier-than-air scouting squadron, VS1D1 which was dedicated to twenty-four-hour anti-submarine patrols during World War II.

Despite its importance in maintaining maritime supremacy during the war (and its primary use as a training field), after Japan's surrender in 1945, the base was scheduled for closure and deactivated in 1946. It appeared the base would have a short history, but the Cold War signaled advancements in both nuclear arms delivery and submarine warfare, bringing new priorities and a new adversary as a past World War II ally became a modern-day opponent.

In 1951, Brunswick Naval Air Station was reactivated, and extensive improvements took place around the station, including a modern control tower, new facilities buildings and dual 8,000-foot runways. By 1959, six patrol squadrons flew both PV2-Neptune and PB4Y-2 Privateer aircraft, conducting constant maritime anti-submarine patrols from the station.[2]

By 1962, the NAS air wing fleet transitioned to P-3A Orion's and continued constant around-the-clock maritime patrols while armed with both conventional and nuclear weapons. These continuous patrols continued for the duration of the Cold War as they kept a constant lookout for Soviet submarines moving beneath the waves.

The P-3 Orion is a maritime patrol, anti-submarine aircraft currently used by different air forces around the world. The aircraft can carry weapons on mounted pylons under its wings as well as in the plane's bomb bay. The aircraft's impressive sensor and imaging systems make it the ideal aircraft for not only submarine hunting, but also for general reconnaissance and search & rescue operations. The aircraft is especially adept at flying both low altitudes and slow speeds, making it an extremely efficient sub hunter.[3]

In addition to continuous anti-submarine patrols, Brunswick NAS also provided support for NASA in 1965 and 1966, aiding in the recovery of both the Mercury and Gemini space capsules. Resident squadrons flew in support of the Vietnam War (1966) and Operation Desert Shield (1990). During the mid-1990s, more than 10,000 officers, enlisted personnel, civilian contractors, and family members occupied the base.

One of only a couple of bases in Maine to survive the closures following the resolution of the Cold War, NAS Brunswick continued to patrol the skies until the Defense Base Realignment and Closure Act of 2005 selected the base for a mandated 2011 closure.[4]

Unlike some of the remote areas where bases were located throughout Maine, Brunswick had a large population to begin with. The coastal Maine community is an idyllic location for business with colleges close by, Bath Iron Works, a thriving nearby commercial fishing industry, and tourism. Even though thousands of military personnel, family members, and civilians were living or working at Brunswick NAS, the sting of the base's closure was not felt as deeply as closures in other Maine communities. Brunswick now has a successful business airport community where the NAS used to be; management and ongoing development of the property is handled by the Midcoast Regional Redevelopment Authority and the area was aptly named Brunswick Landing which is now home to several businesses, Southern Maine Community College, and Brunswick Executive Airport.[5]

For sixty years, U.S. Navy sub hunters flew missions from Brunswick NAS and although most of the station has now been reimagined and redeveloped, remnants of what once was does remain, some in plain sight, some more inconspicuously placed, and more still restricted to any access under federal restrictions. Many restricted areas are part of an Environmental Protection Agency Superfund site and are still being monitored for suspected PFAS and other harmful chemicals.[6]

As a U.S. Navy veteran who was once briefly assigned to Brunswick, it was rather surreal to visit the parts of the base which now stand abandoned and have not been redeveloped.

A mixture of U.S. Navy and RAF planes on the tarmac, 1944. "Visible are Grumman F4F/FM-1 Wildcat fighters, Grumman TBF Avenger torpedo bombers and Vought F4U-1 Corsair fighters. A North American T-6 Texan/Harvard with U.S. markings is visible in the center."[7]

Above left: A damaged RAF plane in for repairs at hangar #3, Brunswick NAS, March 14, 1944.[8]

Above right: RAF Vought Corsair 1 fighters in formation during a transition flight out of Brunswick NAS.[9] *(Photo by Lt. Charles F. Jacobs, 1943)*

Aerial view of Brunswick NAS by the Department of the Navy, 1946.[10]

A P-3 Orion in preparation for takeoff during one of Maine's many winter snowstorms. Regardless of weather, nothing could or would stop the constant patrols out of Brunswick. December 3, 1991.[11]

A Naval Imaging Command photo of a Patrol Squadron 23 (VP-23) P-3C Orion Anti-Submarine Warfare Aircraft flying off the bow of a Soviet Victor III nuclear-powered attack sub. The photograph was taken shortly after the sub was spotted, within 500 miles of the coast, east of Charleston, SC. Date of occurrence, November 11, 1983.[13]

Above left: Even now, fourteen years after the base has closed, you can still get a strong sense of the security that the U.S. Navy had, especially in the weapons storage areas.

Above right: Many bunkers have blast walls in front of them. Common munitions in naval submarine warfare (specific to the P-3 Orion) include both 1,000- and 2,000-pound mines, Mk. 46/50 & 54 torpedoes, AGM-84 Harpoons, AGM-84K SLAM-ER and AGM-65F missiles, and depth bombs.[14]

A large portion of the weapons storage area is now a network of public walking trails. During my visit, I met several people walking with very happy dogs.

Not all the weapons storage facilities are walking areas open to the public. The Explosive Ordinance Disposal (EOD) area is a Superfund site and is closed to the public. The structures built into the earth are three, 3,200-square-foot weapons magazines, built in 1973 in support of the adjacent weapons facility.[15, 16]

The facility was built in 1958 and was the home of the Advanced Undersea Weapons (AUW) shop, with the tin-roofed addition being added in the 1960s. Advanced undersea weapons of the Cold War era included the B-57 nuclear depth bomb which was a variable yield thermonuclear device that delivered up to a 10-kiloton blast. From 1981 until the base closure, the facility operated as the Explosive Ordinance Disposal facility.[17]

The control tower and support building (building 200) were built in 1952, replacing the temporary flight control facilities that were present during World War II. The Brunswick executive airport is now operated as a Class E, non-towered airport, so the U.S. Navy control tower is dormant.

An updated control tower was built in 2004 for around $15 million and was only used by the U.S. Navy for a year before the base closure was announced. Today the tower sits abandoned on the opposite side of the airport from the smaller tower.[18]

Once known by service personnel as the back gate, this gate now has traffic flowing through it unrestricted and armed shore patrol officers no longer screen motorists as they pass by.

17
NAVAL COMPUTER AND TELECOMMUNICATIONS STATION, CUTLER

In 1957, the U.S. Navy acquired more than 3,000 acres of coastal property near the quiet little fishing village of Cutler and began construction on a massive radio and communications station. Four years later, on June 23, 1961, Naval Computer and Telecommunications Station (NCTS) Cutler was commissioned.[1]

Located on the shore of Holmes Bay, the station was constructed to allow naval assets to communicate throughout the Atlantic and Arctic Oceans, and the Mediterranean Sea. Communication with planes and ships had always been a matter of rudimentary radio broadcasting, but to communicate with deployed submarines, the large underwater ships previously had to surface and raise an antenna to communicate, opening the vessels up to detection and leaving them vulnerable. When the Cutler station was built, it allowed for submarines to communicate at depth without surfacing (using encrypted text messages).

The Cutler station once had both very low frequency (VLF) and high frequency (HF) arrays, which were in separate areas of the station property. Although both frequencies are used in electronic communications, the primary reason for the Cutler base, and the star of the proverbial show is the VLF antenna array which dominates the skyline.

Consisting of 35,000 cubic yards of concrete, 15,000 tons of steel, more than 70,000 pounds of bronze conductor material, and over 2,000 miles of copper wire, the station was the first and largest of its kind, generating an impressive 2,000,000 watts of electrical energy.[2] The onsite diesel-powered generators create enough electricity to power the city of Bangor, and the tower array is designed with specialized counterweights that weigh 220 tons each to offset the 100,000-pound pull of the towers. The tower array consists of twenty-six antennas, which range in height from 799 to 997 feet.

In 2000, the U.S. Navy made the decision to close the administrative areas of the base along with the 100-acre high frequency area.

Right: Undated photo which appears to be the late '70s showing the entrance to the station with the administrative areas in the mid-ground and housing in the far background.[3]

Below: In this 2024 photo, the administration building is eerily empty, and the nation's ensign no longer flies at its entrance. The 85-acre administrative area was transferred to the Cutler Development Authority when the base closed.

The perimeter surrounding the inactive high-frequency area is posted with radiation hazard signs and the entire area is closed to public access.

The very low-frequency area still plays an important role in the communication systems of the U.S. Navy, but the area is now maintained and staffed by civilian communication specialists.[5]

18
OVER-THE-HORIZON BACKSCATTER RADAR NETWORK

This long-range radar network was first proposed by the U.S. Air Force in 1966, but development on a prototype did not begin until 1975. However, despite this advanced radar system being an important development of the Cold War, by the time the network was ready to be activated, the Cold War was nearly over.

Maine was the chosen location for the prototype which began testing in 1980. In 1982, a contract was given to build a full-scale model of the prototype at the same location(s). The system was designated AN/FPS-118 and was operational in a limited capacity in 1988; the U.S. Air Force took control of it in 1990.[1]

The Over-the-Horizon Backscatter (OTH-B) radar was an advanced early warning and detection radar system that was created to detect incoming long-range enemy aircraft flying at low altitudes. Conventional radar had historically only had an effective range of around 250 miles, but with the development of the OTH-B, a range of 1,800 miles was achieved. Rather than using straight-line microwave frequencies found in conventional radar, the OTH-B used radio frequencies bounced off the ionosphere to achieve a greater range and detect low-flying inbound aircraft traveling beyond the horizon's line-of-sight.

The system was elaborate with a transmission site in Moscow (Moscow Air Force Station), a receiver site at Columbia Falls (Columbia Falls Air Force Station) and a data processing center in Bangor, at the Bangor Air National Guard Base. In 1990, mere months after the fall of the Berlin Wall, the large radar system became operational. However, it quickly proved to be unnecessary technology due to the diminished threat of Soviet attack and the entire system was placed on caretaker status by the U.S. Air Force on April 18, 1991.[2]

During the early to mid-1990s, the National Oceanic and Atmospheric Administration (NOAA) took advantage of the powerful radar and used it to monitor ocean currents and surface winds. Drug enforcement agencies also used the system to monitor smuggling activities throughout the 1990s, but by 2002, the system was becoming too cumbersome and costly to operate, and after NORAD stated there was no operational requirement for the OTH-B radar network, Columbia Falls AFS and Moscow AFS were closed.[3]

Today, most all evidence of Moscow AFS has been removed, and the property has been repurposed and redeveloped. A small wind farm is now occupying a portion of the property and there is little evidence of the large OTH-B transmitting station that once occupied the area.

Columbia Falls AFS still remains largely intact at least regarding the structures and some hardware. All the computers, processors, antennas, etc. were taken away when the U.S. Air Force vacated. Unfortunately, the secluded location of the station, a recreational vehicle trail that runs through it, and a high summer transient population on the nearby blueberry fields, have all created the perfect storm for what has been left behind. What is not spray-painted over with graffiti has been senselessly smashed or viciously vandalized.

Above: The immense space that the Columbia Falls AFS occupies is difficult to convey with a simple photograph. The entire receiver area consisted of the main station and two sub-stations, each nearly a mile apart from one another. Please make note of the helipad in the foreground.[4]

Below: With the helipad still in the foreground, this 2024 aerial perspective helps to capture the magnitude of the site. The antenna fencing and radar towers are now gone but its size is still quite impressive.

The control area/entrance of the main complex. This building is the largest out of the three station facilities.[5]

Interior, front entrance main complex, 2024. This station represents an important technological advancement during the late Cold War era, especially considering it was both the prototype OTH-B location, and one of the first fully functioning stations.

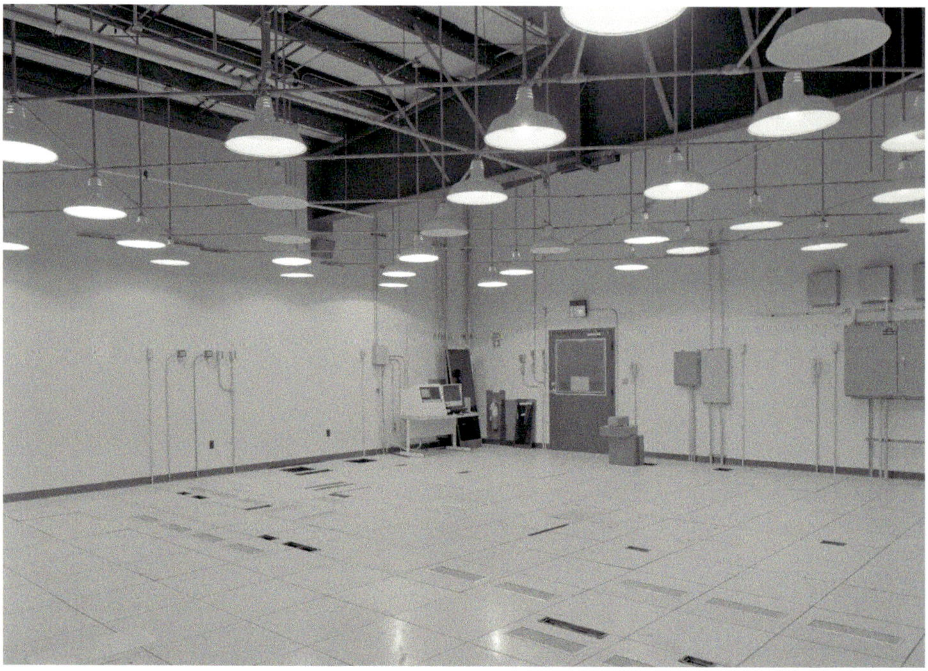

A computer room inside the main building. The room had a raised floor and halon fire suppression systems.[6]

The same room in 2024. This room is deep in the main complex building and it is apparent that most of the computer and electronic equipment were situated in this building.

To offer a better perspective of the size of Columbia Falls AFS, follow the road from Complex-Section 2 (in the foreground) until the road turns to the right. Then follow it along to the right and you will notice the tiny blue speck of the main complex. Mind you, only two of the three complex sections are represented in this image.

A broken sign for building 202 lies outside of the perimeter fence. The Air Force, Tactical Air Command emblem is still in the upper left-hand corner.

CONCLUSION

Not so long ago in Maine's history, coastal artillery gunners manned their posts in the dead of night while giving themselves the constant reminder that the threat of an enemy approach would not evade the vigilant. Now, spotters no longer need to peer out into pea-soup thick fog from the tops of towers as they try and discern the difference between the lights of approaching enemy ships and the occasional star peeking through the eerie mist.

No longer are planes fueling on the tarmac in below-freezing temperatures while crews prepare to fly into a nor'easter searching for submarines prowling beneath ink-black Atlantic waters. The only thing that would differentiate the turbulent seas from the dark night skies were the constant 12-foot rollers, creating whitecaps that looked like mass herds of aquatic sheep leaping across the seas.

From sailing ships to submarines, throughout the State's 205-year history, Maine has seen its share of military development and defensive strongholds, but the missile bases and coastal artillery forts are gone, communications centers and submarine detection stations are closed, and the heavy-bomber bases loaded with nuclear weapons have all disappeared. Now only traces are left behind in spaces occupied by the Air National Guard and other civilian entities such as Bangor International Airport. It begs one to consider the notion of what might be next for the State of Maine. A world of peace is certainly a pacifist's dream, but unfortunately it goes against the history of human nature. The securing of our borders has been a concern for our species since we first developed the concept of borders, so the future remains to be seen.

The social and economic impact of the coming and going of these facilities ranges from minor to vast, depending on the location and demographic. In Aroostook County, residents are still feeling the sting that was felt with the closure of Loring and its surrounding support facilities, nearly thirty-one years after the base closure. The rise and fall of Strategic Air Command has left a profound impact on the area.

In contrast, consider regions such as Portland and its neighbor Brunswick. Consider the area's fishing and tourist industries, accompanied with the education centers and the area's proximity to Boston. The opening and closing of military facilities have impacted these areas far less significantly than the northernmost region of the state.

In Down East Maine (that portion that begins in Ellsworth and continues east to Eastport) the impact is more varied. The region near Acadia National Park experienced a gain when it acquired Otter Cliffs, Schoodic Point, and other properties. Acadia National Park sees annual visitation of over four million people, so the communities in the Mount Desert Island region prosper with or without the military. In contrast, the region around Cutler saw a larger economic loss and fewer gains with the departure of the U.S. Navy.

Environmental concerns are also present statewide. The Environment Protection Agency has established areas of multiple bases as Superfund sites due to issues ranging from radiation contaminated dirt to asbestos mitigation. Current concerns such as the recent discovery of PFAS chemicals (polyfluoroalkyl substances) in areas of Limestone, Brunswick, and Cutler have created investigations which remain ongoing.

Development is certainly the best a community can hope for, but the preservation of our history remains a concern as well. What warrants preservation and what is it about some of these places that they become doomed to a slow decay as they fade from our memories? The best examples being the preservation of Naval Security Group Activity (NSGA) Winter Harbor, while its station to the east on the Corea peninsula has been condemned to a slow decay.

Regardless of the fate of these facilities, they all deserve to be remembered as proud parts of our history as the State of Maine fought to defend its borders and stood vigil on its watch to defend the United States. It is fortunate that we have various historical societies, preservation groups and museums that have dedicated themselves to preserving the memory of places such as the facilities featured in this book. During the research for this book, I was fortunate to have worked with several organizations that went above and beyond in helping to locate historic documents and photographs; I will provide a list in the citations with the hopeful recommendation that you support them with a visit; either online or perhaps on a history trip of your own in the great State of Maine.

ENDNOTES

Dedications and Acknowledgments

1 The official photograph of Chief Canine Sinbad (U.S. Coast Guard).
2 Chidlow, N. L., "The Long Blue Line: Chief Canine Sinbad," August 26, 2022.

Chapter 1

1 Monroe, J., "Second Inaugural Address of James Monroe," March 5, 1821.
2 "Fort Scammell" starforts.com/scammell.html. Accessed December 1, 2024.
3 Quint, R., "The Battle of Portland Harbor (Conclusion)," *Emerging Civil War*, February 12, 2015.
4 Bennett, T. R., "Civil War soldier executed in Maine for desertion may have been disabled," *Bangor Daily News*, September 25, 2023.
5 Jordan, W. B., *Red Diamond Regiment* (White Mane Publishing Company, 1996), p. 84.
6 United States Army Signal Corps, Photographer, "Fort Preble Aerial B18145002," *c.* 1936.

Chapter 2

1 Peladeu, M. B., and Reed, R. G., *The Kennebec Arsenal* (Historic Preservation Commission Documents, 1997), p. 7.
2 *Ibid.*, p. 10.
3 *Ibid.*, p. 11.
4 Mills Farm, A., "2013 Most Endangered," Maine Preservation, January 7, 2019.
5 "Kennebec Arsenal" *Meander Maine*, 2020.
6 Edwards, K., "Augusta declares historic Kennebec Arsenal property dangerous," *Kennebec Journal*, August 7, 2022.
7 National Archives, 1828, NAID:205135296.

Chapter 4

1 "Editorial on Potential fifth column activities," *Houlton Pioneer Times,* June 20, 1940.
2 "War Department officially announced the purchase of the Houlton airport," Houlton *Pioneer Times*, August 14, 1941.
3 "Acting base commander," *Houlton Pioneer Times,* December 11, 1941.
4 Arel, J. J., "The History of Houlton Army Airfield," Archives of Cary Library, Houlton, Maine.

Chapter 5

1 National Park Service, "The Endicott Era Defenses," February 26, 2015.
2 Bradley, Ph.D., R. L., *The Forts of Maine, 1607–1945* (1981), pp. 36-37, courtesy of the Maine Historic Preservation Commission.
3 *Ibid.*, p. 37.
4 "Historical Fort McKinley and Great Diamond Island," Fort McKinley Museum.
5 United States Army Signal Corps, Photographer, "M1835", *c.* 1936, cdsg.org.
6 *Ibid.*, Fort Popham.
7 *Ibid.*, McKinley.
8 Fort McKinley, ME., Post Hospital Postcard, *c.* 1912, scanned from author's private collection.

Chapter 6

1 Urban, S., J01, "End of an Era NNS020321-08," *Navy NewsStand*, March 21, 2002.
2 Lee III, J. J., "U.S. Naval Radio Station-Apartment Building, Historic Structure Report" *NPS*, 2009, p. 36.
3 *Ibid.*, p. 31.
4 Chief of Naval Operations, "Disestablishment of Naval Security Group Activity Winter Harbor, Maine," U.S. Navy OPNAVNOTE 5450, March 18, 2002.
5 National Archives, 1919. NAID: 6210474.
6 National Archives, 1939. NAID: 38328341.
7 National Archives, *c.* 1965. NAID: 38328325.
8 "Aerial Photo: A5697-28-2," *Maine Geological Survey Aerial Photos*, July 8, 1997.
9 "Classic Wizard," U.S Naval Cryptologic Veterans Association, usncva.org, date unknown.
10 "The Elephant Cage," U.S Naval Cryptologic Veterans Association, usncva.org.

Chapter 8

1 U.S. Air Force, "Bangor Salutes Dow AFB," C. F. Boone Nationwide Publications, Inc., 1964. p. 3.
2 Thompson, A. G., *A Brief History of Dow Field* (1946).
3 Garbinski, J. C., *The United States Air Force in Maine* (The Maine Aviation Historical Society, 1998), p. 3.
4 "AIR-2 Missile," Air Force Armament Museum Foundation.
5 Garbinski, J. C., *The United States Air Force in Maine*, p. 11.
6 Parsch, A., "Directory of U.S. Military Rockets and Missiles."
7 National Archives, 1956. NAID: 75747601.
8 National Archives, 1957. NAID:77821449.
9 "Bangor Salutes Dow AFB," p. 12.
10 "Aerial Photo: DOTOO-APT-77," Maine Geological Survey Aerial Photos, August 28, 2000.
11 National Archives, 1959. NAID: 77821511
12 "Aerial Photo: 38487," Maine Geological Survey Aerial Photos, May 7, 1963.
13 National Archives, 1959. NAID: 280957196
14 BOMARC, National Museum of the U.S. Air Force, 090603-F-1234P-002.

Chapter 9

1 Winkler, D. F., *Searching the Skies: The Legacy of the United States Cold War Defense Radar Program* (USACERL, June 1997), p. 24.
2 *Ibid.*, p. 26.

Chapter 10

1 "SAGE: Semi-automatic Ground Environment Air Defense System: Software Development."
2 "SAGE: Semi-Automatic Ground Environment Air Defense System," Lincoln Laboratory MIT.

Chapter 11

1 "765 Radar Squadron (SAGE) 32nd Air Division Unit Yearbook 1955."
2 "Charleston Air Force Station Formerly Used Defense Site," U.S. Army Engineers.
3 "766 Radar Squadron (SAGE) 32nd Air Division Unit Yearbook 1955."
4 National Archives, 1961. NAID: 77821385.
5 "Final Community Relations Plan, W912WJ-19-D-0002 TASK ORDER F0182" U.S. Army Corps of Engineers, September 16, 2020.

Chapter 12

1 "907 Radar Squadron (SAGE) 32nd Air Division Unit Yearbook 1955."
2 Phillips, A. D., "907 Radar Squadron #265," *c.* 1960s, scanned postcard from author's private collection.
3 *Ibid.*, 121.
4 Heller, R. J., "Water remediation," *The Quoddy Tides*, December 23, 2016, pp. 1, 14.

Chapter 13

1 Ingles, H. D., "What Was the SAGE System?"
2 "SAGE: Semi-Automatic Ground Environment Air Defense System: Software Development," Lincoln Laboratory MIT.
3 "SAGE: Semi-Automatic Ground Environment Air Defense System: The AN/FSQ-7 Computer," Lincoln Laboratory MIT.
4 Owen, L., "Brunswick, Maine, Region," *Owen Art-Color*, *c.* 1965, scanned postcard from author's private collection.
5 Stanton, J., "Stewart SAGE Direction Center," June 8, 2016.

Chapter 14

1 Ward, W. W., and Naka, F. R., "Long-Range UHF Radars for Ground Control of Airborne Interceptors," 2001.
2 Myers, A., "Radar Tower-Redux," *The Middle Ground* (West Bath Historical Society, Fall 2012).

Chapter 15

1 Winkler, D. F., "Searching the Skies, ND94-0416," USAF Headquarters Air Combat Command, June 1997, p. 82.
2 *Ibid.*, p. 36.
3 "Changing of the Guard," The Budd Company Ad, *Time* magazine, January 19, 1962, p. 76.

Chapter 16

1 "R.N.A.S. Brunswick," Royal Navy Archives.
2 "Former Naval Air Station Brunswick," NAVFAC.

3 Bernier, R., "The Sub Hunter," *Air & Space Quarterly*, Winter 2025.
4 "Former Naval Air Station Brunswick," NAVFAC.
5 Carrigan, D., "10 years after the Navy, former base has bounced back," News Center Maine, May 26, 2021.
6 "Brunswick Naval Air Station Cleanup Activities," EPA.
7 National Archives, 1944. NAID: 6254888.
8 National Archives, 1944. NAID: 6254891.
9 Jacobs, Lt. C. F, "Vought Corsair I Fighters 80-G-473440," Naval History and Heritage Command, 1939–1945.
10 National Archives. NAID: 38330071.
11 National Archives, 1991. NAID: 6479495.
12 National Archives, 1991. NAID: 6479500.
13 National Archives, 1983. NAID: 6383488.
14 P-3C Orion, navair.navy.mil/product/P-3C-Orion.
15 Studlien, S., "Second Five-Year Review Report (1999–2004) for the Naval Air Station, Brunswick, Maine NPL Site letter," United States EPA, September 29, 2005.
16 NAVFAC Former NAS Brunswick, Restoration Advisory Board Meeting, June 14, 2012.
17 "Former Naval Air Station Brunswick," NAVFAC.
18 Swinconeck, J., "MRRA awaits deed to tower," *Times Record*, July 17, 2014.

Chapter 17

1 "Cutler Naval Telecommunications Station," Maine, The Center for Land Use Interpretation.
2 Crane, J., "Place of the Tall Towers," *Downeast Magazine*, January 1961.
3 "Naval Communication Unit Cutler," navy-radio.com.
4 Kryszak, J., "Residents near Cutler Navy base struggle with 'forever chemicals' in water," *Portland Press Herald*, May 21, 2023.
5 Smith, T., "A new coastal community," Mainebiz, August 21, 2006.

Chapter 18

1 Historic American Engineering Record, "Over-the-Horizon Backscatter Radar Network," Library of Congress, Control Number me0380.
2 Winkler, D. F., "Searching the Skies, ND94-0416," USAF Headquarters Air Combat Command, June 1997, p. 60.
3 "Columbia Falls Air Force Station," Maine, The Center for Land Use Interpretation.
4 "Over-the-Horizon Backscatter Radar Network," Library of Congress, Control Number me0384.
5 *Ibid.*, me0380.
6 *Ibid.*, me0380.

FURTHER READING, HISTORICAL SOCIETIES, & MUSEUMS

Aroostook County Historical and Art Museum, www.houltonmuseum.org/_
Foley, Jr., G. F., *Sinbad of the Coast Guard* (Dodd, Mead & Company, 1945)
Fort McKinley Museum, fortmckinleymuseum.weebly.com/
Garbinski, J. C., *The United States Air Force in Maine* (Maine Aviation Historical Society, 2000)
Kennebec Historical Society, www.kennebechistorical.org/
Maine Aviation Historical Society/Maine Air Museum, www.maineairmuseum.com/
Maine Historical Society, www.mainehistory.org/
Maine Preservation Commission, www.maine.gov/mhpc/home
Thibodeau, A. T., *The Aroostook Arms Race: Cold War in the Crown of Maine* (America Through Time, 2025)